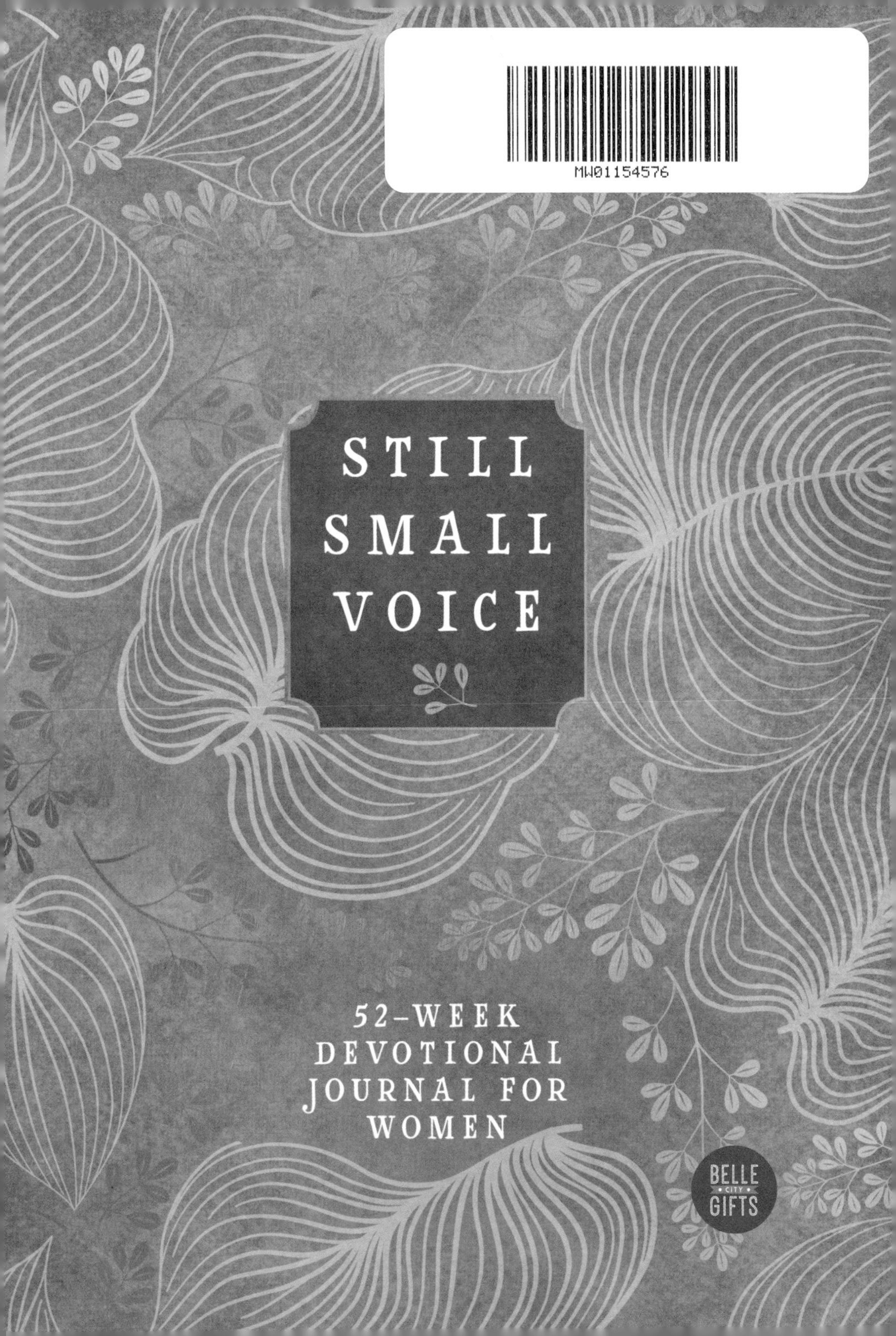
MW01154576
STILL SMALL VOICE
52-WEEK DEVOTIONAL JOURNAL FOR WOMEN
BELLE CITY GIFTS

Belle City Gifts
Savage, Minnesota, USA
Belle City Gifts is an imprint of BroadStreet Publishing Group, LLC.
Broadstreetpublishing.com

STILL SMALL VOICE

9781424570393

Typesetting and design by Garborg Design Works | garborgdesign.com

Compiled and edited by Michelle Winger | literallyprecise.com

Printed in China.

25 26 27 28 29 30 31 7 6 5 4 3 2 1

The LORD was not in the wind...

the LORD was not in the earthquake...

the LORD was not in the fire;

and after the fire a still small voice.

1 KINGS 19:11-12 NKJV

INTRODUCTION

How do you hear God's voice? Very few of us experience him speaking audibly. More often we hear him in the quiet. In the stillness. In the moments we are searching for answers and taking the time to listen. But he also speaks to us through his Word.

This beautifully designed devotional journal for women features meditations on the words of Jesus, spoken when he walked the earth. Thought-provoking prompts and questions and encouraging Scriptures will help your weekly devotional life to be focused and intentional. As you quiet yourself and meditate on the words of Jesus, you will discover the many facets of his character.

Reflect on the promises of God and express your thoughts, prayers, and praise in the space provided. Experience his goodness, faithfulness, compassion, and perfect peace. Pray with a heart full of gratitude and hope, confident that he is ever near, listening with a tender heart of compassion and ready to answer you in his still small voice.

WEEK 1

PERSONAL INVITATION

"Come, follow me."

JOHN 1:43 NLT

Just as Jesus invited his disciples, so he says to you, "Come, follow me." Have you taken him up on his offer? Have you left your comfort zone and old way of doing things? Have you let yourself be drawn to his wonders and kindness?

Following Jesus transforms your life. When you take in his wisdom and let his perspective challenge your preconceived notions, your old way of thinking will feel inadequate. There is much to discover in the journey of knowing him. Will you receive his kindness and move toward him? Though the details of your future are unknown, the character of Christ will never change as you travel with him as your friend, healer, teacher, and savior. There is both mystery and hope; there is peace and expectation. Your heart's curiosity can lead you closer to the one who calls you.

REFLECTION

How can you choose to follow God not knowing what that will look like in every circumstance or season? Do you trust his character? Do you want to know him more?

My Thoughts

After reflecting on this devotion and follow-up questions, here are my thoughts.

My Response

This is how I can apply the message to my life.

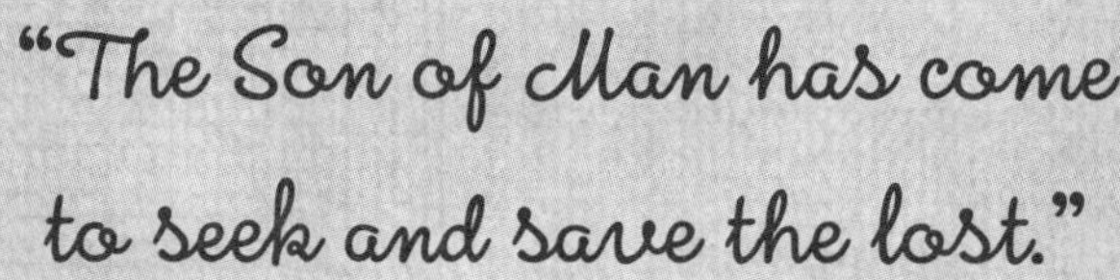

"The Son of Man has come
to seek and save the lost."

LUKE 19:10 CSB

To me, this Scripture feels most like (check one)

☐ A PROMISE ☐ AN INSTRUCTION ☐ A TRUTH

Here's how it impacts me...

PRAYER

GRATITUDE

I have been blessed with so many good things.
Here is what I am particularly thankful for this week.

REQUESTS

After reading and reflecting, here is what I'm asking God for.

WEEK 2

EVERY LITTLE THING

"Even the very hairs of your head are all numbered."

MATTHEW 10:30 NIV

God knows not only our names and ages but every detail about us. He cares deeply about the smallest aspects of life. Jesus illustrated this by saying he knows the number of hairs on our heads. It's such a specific, nearly impossible thing to know, yet he takes notice of things that seem absurd to us. There are no limits to his understanding.

Why worry with a detailed and loving God overlooking our lives? Let's put our wholehearted trust in him and turn over our anxieties to his patient presence. He is enough to sustain us, and he will provide what we need. Every little thing is covered by him.

REFLECTION

Thank God for his detailed attention and care for you. How can you trust him with what you can't control or anticipate? How will you rest in him this week?

My Thoughts

After reflecting on this devotion and follow-up questions, here are my thoughts.

My Response

This is how I can apply the message to my life.

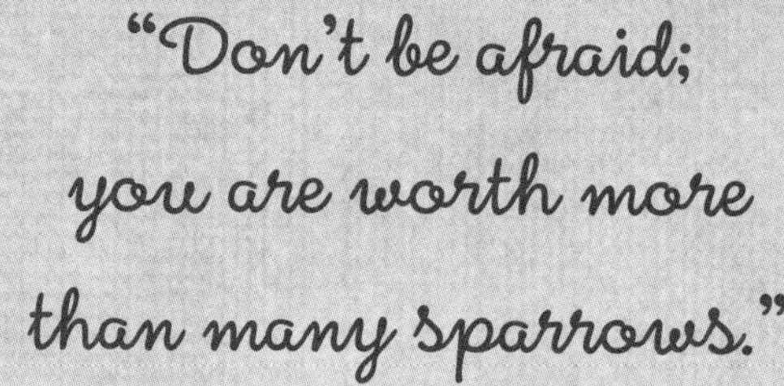

"Don't be afraid;
you are worth more
than many sparrows."

LUKE 12:7 NIV

To me, this Scripture feels most like (check one)

☐ A PROMISE ☐ AN INSTRUCTION ☐ A TRUTH

Here's how it impacts me...

PRAYER

GRATITUDE

I have been blessed with so many good things.

Here is what I am particularly thankful for this week.

REQUESTS

After reading and reflecting, here is what I'm asking God for.

WEEK 3

TRUSTWORTHY

"Whoever can be trusted with a little can also be trusted with a lot, and whoever is dishonest with a little is dishonest with a lot."

LUKE 16:10 NCV

Jesus is talking about money here, but the principle applies to all areas of life. When we have resources that could benefit others instead of us, it takes integrity, self-discipline, and honor to do the right thing. Honesty paired with reliability is powerful. Whoever can be trusted with a little will earn trust with more.

Think of Joseph from the Old Testament. He was sold into slavery by his brothers, and everything was taken from him. However, that was only the beginning of his story. He was as trustworthy as they come. Proving himself a hard, reliable, and honest worker, he rose through the ranks to become trusted advisor to the king. He started with nothing, but he ended up being one of the most powerful men in Egypt.

REFLECTION

How do you live with integrity before God and before others. How can you honor God and those who trust you, regardless of how little or how much you have?

My Thoughts

After reflecting on this devotion and follow-up questions, here are my thoughts.

My Response

This is how I can apply the message to my life.

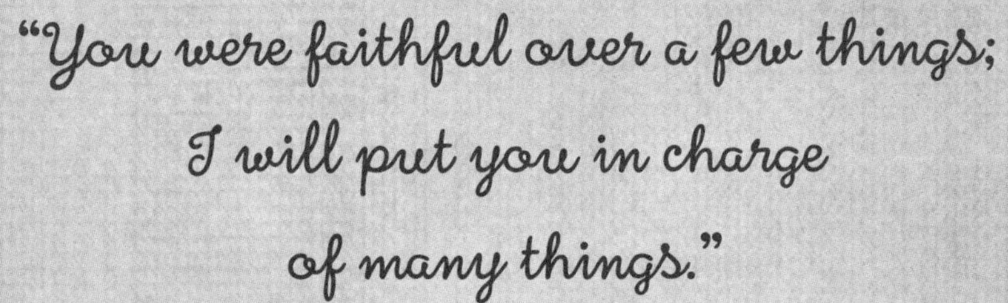

“You were faithful over a few things; I will put you in charge of many things.”

MATTHEW 25:21 CSB

To me, this Scripture feels most like (check one)

☐ A PROMISE ☐ AN INSTRUCTION ☐ A TRUTH

Here’s how it impacts me…

PRAYER

GRATITUDE

I have been blessed with so many good things.
Here is what I am particularly thankful for this week.

REQUESTS

After reading and reflecting, here is what I'm asking God for.

WEEK 4

FORGIVENESS

When Jesus saw their faith, he said to the paralyzed man, "Son, your sins are forgiven."

MARK 2:5 NIV

Before Jesus healed the paralyzed man, he did something even more powerful; he removed his guilt, shame, and fear. On behalf of the Father, he forgave the man's sins. The Pharisees balked at this. They wanted to know what authority gave Jesus the right to do such a thing. In Jewish law, cleansing sacrifices needed to be offered in strict ways by specific people. Jesus broke the mold by releasing the man from guilt. Why and how did he do this? Because he is the Son of God, and he came to set captives free.

What God does not hold against us, may we refuse to hold against each other or ourselves. May we liberate others with our forgiveness. Only God can remove our guilt, and Jesus Christ has already done that. We can trust him and let his mercy empower our acts of forgiveness. What we let go of, we can leave to the Lord. We are alive and free in his mercy!

REFLECTION

Thank God for his forgiveness. How does it feel to know you are set free from the guilt and shame that comes with imperfection?

My Thoughts

After reflecting on this devotion and follow-up questions, here are my thoughts.

My Response

This is how I can apply the message to my life.

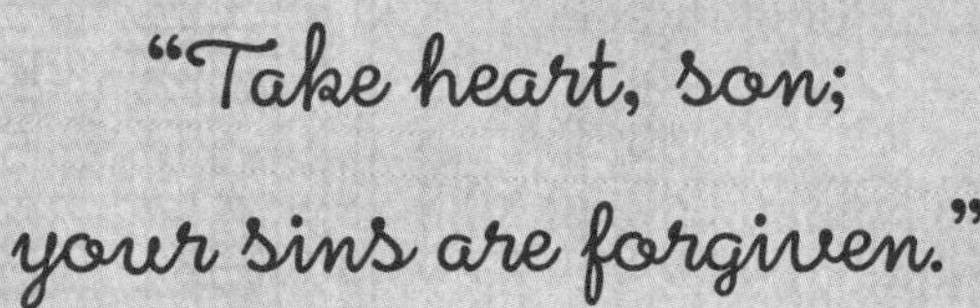

"Take heart, son;
your sins are forgiven."

MATTHEW 9:2 NIV

To me, this Scripture feels most like (check one)

☐ A PROMISE ☐ AN INSTRUCTION ☐ A TRUTH

Here's how it impacts me...

PRAYER

GRATITUDE

I have been blessed with so many good things.
Here is what I am particularly thankful for this week.

REQUESTS

After reading and reflecting, here is what I'm asking God for.

WEEK 5

TRUST HIM

> When he had finished speaking, he said to Simon, "Now go out where it is deeper, and let down your nets to catch some fish."
>
> LUKE 5:4 NLT

In return for letting him use his boat as a place to teach the crowds from, Jesus gave Simon Peter a gift. Though Simon had just returned from fishing all night without any luck, Jesus told him to row out into deeper water and cast his nets. Simon was skeptical, but he did as Jesus instructed.

When Simon pulled up the nets, they were ready to burst from the load of fish they held! Simon Peter's response was remarkably humble. Knowing the state of his heart and life, he told Jesus to leave him. He did not feel worthy of Jesus' attention. Even so, we know that Jesus would eventually build his church on the rock of Peter. He was one of the forefathers of Christianity. Don't count yourself out when Jesus wants to teach you to walk in the power of his ways. There is no one better to trust.

REFLECTION

God is so good! Let yourself be astounded by his love. Choose to follow him and allow his kindness to draw you in. How will you surrender to his leadership?

My Thoughts

After reflecting on this devotion and follow-up questions, here are my thoughts.

My Response

This is how I can apply the message to my life.

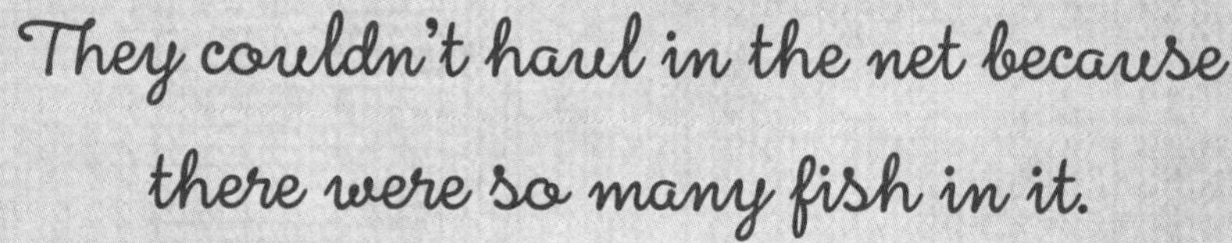

They couldn't haul in the net because there were so many fish in it.

JOHN 21:6 NLT

To me, this Scripture feels most like (check one)

☐ A PROMISE ☐ AN INSTRUCTION ☐ A TRUTH

Here's how it impacts me...

PRAYER

GRATITUDE

I have been blessed with so many good things.
Here is what I am particularly thankful for this week.

REQUESTS

After reading and reflecting, here is what I'm asking God for.

WEEK 6

WAIT ON HIM

> Once when he was eating with them, he commanded them, "Do not leave Jerusalem until the Father sends you the gift he promised, as I told you before."
>
> ACTS 1:4 NLT

Sometimes we need to move ahead in life. Other times, waiting is necessary. Why would we rush ahead in our own strength when God offers us the strength of his Spirit to empower us? When he tells you to wait, listen. There is purpose in all he does.

The Holy Spirit is a generous gift. Fellowship with the Spirit infuses our inner beings with peace, love, joy, endurance, and hope. The fruit of the Spirit can be witnessed in the lives of those submitted to him. The Holy Spirit transforms us from the inside out and gives us all we need to experience the fullness of God's life within us. Take time to wait on the Lord each day and ask the Holy Spirit to fill you with what you need to thrive in every circumstance and challenge.

REFLECTION

You can be filled with the gift of the Holy Spirit. How will you choose to wait on him today? What else can you set aside to make room for the fruit of the Spirit in your life?

My Thoughts

After reflecting on this devotion and follow-up questions, here are my thoughts.

My Response

This is how I can apply the message to my life.

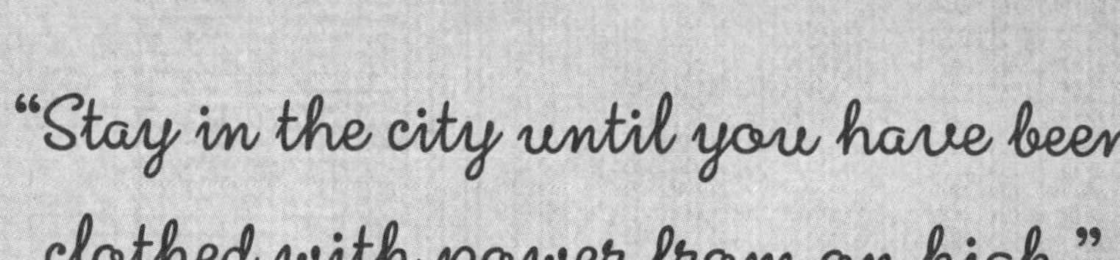

"Stay in the city until you have been clothed with power from on high."

LUKE 24:49 NIV

To me, this Scripture feels most like (check one)

☐ A PROMISE ☐ AN INSTRUCTION ☐ A TRUTH

Here's how it impacts me...

PRAYER

GRATITUDE

I have been blessed with so many good things.
Here is what I am particularly thankful for this week.

REQUESTS

After reading and reflecting, here is what I'm asking God for.

WEEK 7

RELEASE YOUR WORRIES

> "Let not your hearts be troubled. Believe in God; believe also in me."
>
> JOHN 14:1 ESV

We can't escape the troubles of the world, but we can keep our hearts tethered to the one who does the heavy lifting of our burdens. Jesus is marvelous in mercy; he is generous in grace and compassion. He offers us the shelter of a faithful friend. He extends the same safety that a reliable parent does to their child.

What is troubling your heart today? Instead of surrendering to fear, can you surrender it to the Lord? Jesus Christ is capable of carrying all your concerns, and he will not forget to provide for your needs. Will you trust him? Will you take him at his Word and allow his peace to permeate your heart? He is close. Lean in and let go.

REFLECTION

Don't carry the weight of your worries. You will only suffer under the weight of them. How can you give God your fear, anxiety, and concerns, and receive his rest, peace, and help in their place?

My Thoughts

After reflecting on this devotion and follow-up questions, here are my thoughts.

My Response

This is how I can apply the message to my life.

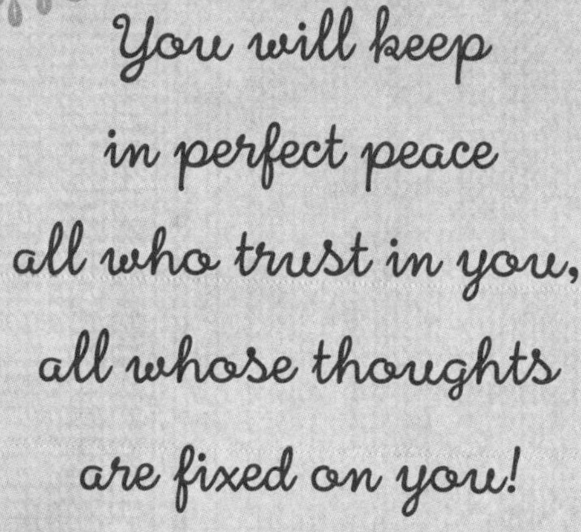

You will keep
in perfect peace
all who trust in you,
all whose thoughts
are fixed on you!

ISAIAH 26:3 NLT

To me, this Scripture feels most like (check one)

☐ A PROMISE ☐ AN INSTRUCTION ☐ A TRUTH

Here's how it impacts me...

PRAYER

GRATITUDE

I have been blessed with so many good things.
Here is what I am particularly thankful for this week.

REQUESTS

After reading and reflecting, here is what I'm asking God for.

WEEK 8

FREE TO GROW

"Others are like the seed planted among the thorny weeds. They hear the teaching, but the worries of this life, the temptation of wealth, and many other evil desires keep the teaching from growing and producing fruit in their lives."

MARK 4:18-19 NCV

Is something stunting your spiritual growth? What keeps you from developing in faith? What thoughts, desires, or fears entangle your mind and heart? We are human, and we all fall short of the glory of God. Fortunately, it doesn't matter how long you have followed the Lord; he always offers more grace when you turn to him.

Think of things that deplete your hope and belief. Conversely, what are the things that (and the people who) infuse you with peace and hope? Whatever is leeching the life out of you, offer it to the Lord. Whatever fills you with the liberating love and life of the Lord, give it more of your attention. When you are free from thorny weeds, you will produce powerful fruit from the Spirit's life within you.

REFLECTION

Is your life producing God's abundant fruit? What limiting beliefs are you holding onto? Ask God to disentangle you with his liberating love and powerful wisdom.

My Thoughts

After reflecting on this devotion and follow-up questions, here are my thoughts.

My Response

This is how I can apply the message to my life.

The world and everything that people want in it are passing away, but the person who does what God wants lives forever.

1 JOHN 2:17 NCV

To me, this Scripture feels most like (check one)

☐ A PROMISE ☐ AN INSTRUCTION ☐ A TRUTH

Here's how it impacts me…

PRAYER

GRATITUDE

I have been blessed with so many good things.
Here is what I am particularly thankful for this week.

REQUESTS

After reading and reflecting, here is what I'm asking God for.

WEEK 9

NOTHING TO HIDE

"Be on your guard against the yeast of the Pharisees, which is hypocrisy. There is nothing concealed that will not be disclosed, or hidden that will not be made known."

LUKE 12:1-2 NIV

Hypocrisy is requiring a certain standard while living by a different measure. It means claiming to value one thing while not following through with actions to support it. Pride can lead us to hypocrisy if we're not careful. It affords grace to us while limiting it for others, and this is not the way of Jesus.

God knows our hearts. He judges not just what others see but the true intentions of a person. When we yield our hearts to Christ, his mercy washes us. He removes the stain of our guilt. Then, we get to extend that gracious compassion to others. May we live as true, honest, and honorable followers of Christ with nothing to hide.

REFLECTION

Have you submitted to the work of Christ in your life? Don't withhold anything from him; he knows so much better than you do. How can you live as someone who is trustworthy, reliable, and completely surrendered to God?

My Thoughts

After reflecting on this devotion and follow-up questions, here are my thoughts.

My Response

This is how I can apply the message to my life.

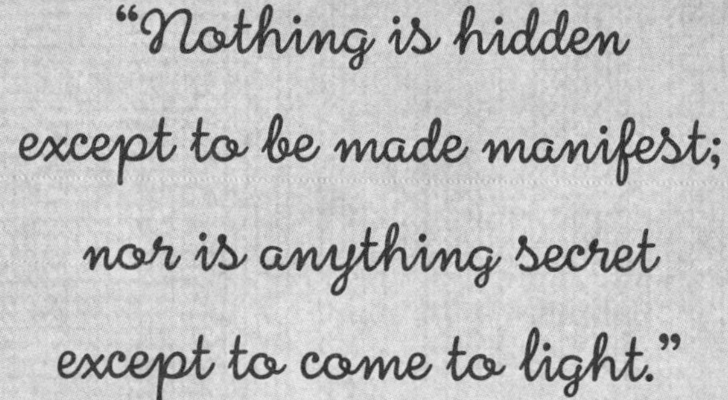

"Nothing is hidden
except to be made manifest;
nor is anything secret
except to come to light."

MARK 4:22 ESV

To me, this Scripture feels most like (check one)

☐ A PROMISE ☐ AN INSTRUCTION ☐ A TRUTH

Here's how it impacts me...

PRAYER

GRATITUDE

I have been blessed with so many good things.
Here is what I am particularly thankful for this week.

REQUESTS

After reading and reflecting, here is what I'm asking God for.

WEEK 10

THE FATHER'S WORK

"I tell you the truth, the Son can do nothing alone.
The Son only does what he sees the Father doing,
because the Son does whatever the Father does."

JOHN 5:19 NCV

Today's verse holds a powerful statement from Jesus; he said he did nothing on his own initiative. Every person he healed, every merciful act he performed, every prayer he prayed, he did to represent the heart and will of the Father.

If you are familiar with the goodness of Christ, you are familiar with the goodness of the Father. The earth is full of the glory of the Lord, and Jesus reminded people of this. The glory of God, more powerful than we can imagine, is also indescribably beautiful. What causes wonder to rise in our hearts or hope to take root? As we look at the ministry of Jesus, as we soak in the wonders of his recorded Word, may awe lead us into deeper fellowship with Spirit, Son, and Father. They are one, and they are accessible even now.

REFLECTION

How would you describe the wonder in your heart when you consider God's goodness? How can you pursue knowing God in deeper ways? Ask him to reveal more of his incredible nature as you turn to him this week.

My Thoughts

After reflecting on this devotion and follow-up questions, here are my thoughts.

My Response

This is how I can apply the message to my life.

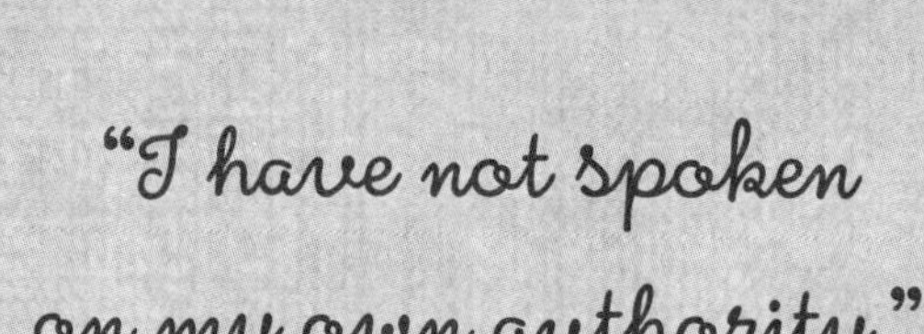

"I have not spoken on my own authority."

JOHN 12:49 ESV

To me, this Scripture feels most like (check one)

☐ A PROMISE ☐ AN INSTRUCTION ☐ A TRUTH

Here's how it impacts me...

PRAYER

GRATITUDE

I have been blessed with so many good things.
Here is what I am particularly thankful for this week.

REQUESTS

After reading and reflecting, here is what I'm asking God for.

WEEK 11

HIDDEN TREASURE

> "The kingdom of heaven is like a treasure hidden in a field. One day a man found the treasure, and then he hid it in the field again. He was so happy that he went and sold everything he owned to buy that field."
>
> MATTHEW 13:44 NCV

Imagine finding a secret treasure no one else had uncovered. What would you do? Would you take it all, leave some behind, or look for the rights to it? The kingdom of God is more glorious, fulfilling, and promising than golden treasure. When we find it, we are encouraged to give all we have to gain the rights to it.

When we surrender ourselves to Christ, we let go of what no longer serves us and receive what he offers. What he offers is far better than anything we leave behind. Do you trust that Jesus is as good as the Word of God says? Spend time in his presence today and ask him to reveal the glorious treasure of his kingdom. Seek and you will find.

REFLECTION

What are you seeking for? Have you found the incredible treasure of Christ? What would you give up to experience this treasure fully?

My Thoughts

After reflecting on this devotion and follow-up questions, here are my thoughts.

My Response

This is how I can apply the message to my life.

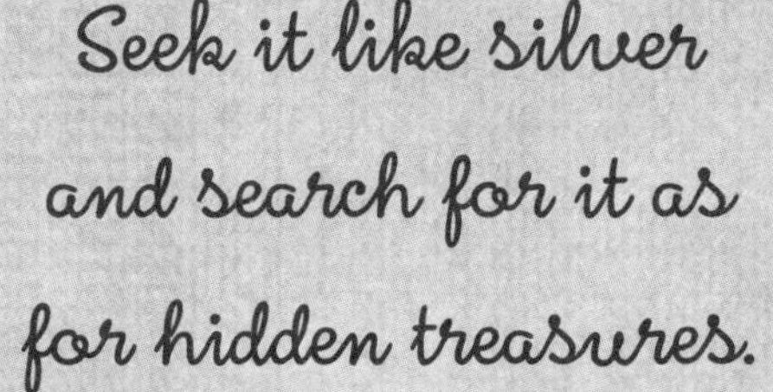
Seek it like silver
and search for it as
for hidden treasures.

PROVERBS 2:4 ESV

To me, this Scripture feels most like (check one)

☐ A PROMISE ☐ AN INSTRUCTION ☐ A TRUTH

Here's how it impacts me...

PRAYER

GRATITUDE

I have been blessed with so many good things.
Here is what I am particularly thankful for this week.

REQUESTS

After reading and reflecting, here is what I'm asking God for.

WEEK 12

POWER OF PEACE

> He got up and rebuked the wind and said to the sea, "Hush, be still." And the wind died down and it became perfectly calm.
>
> MARK 4:39 NASB

Jesus had the power to calm raging seas when he walked this earth, and he still has that power today. He does not defeat storms by raging louder than they do; he speaks peace to the wind and waves, and they calm in response. Instead of relying on shows of brute force to face the storms of life, we can follow Jesus' lead and release peace.

What comes to mind when you think of peacekeepers? Do you imagine them weak? Or do you recognize the power of meeting chaos, trouble, and pressure without threats of violence? This isn't the only time Jesus displayed peace in chaos. When the guards came to take him away in the garden of Gethsemane, his disciples drew their weapons and fought. Jesus told them to put their swords away. Are we brave enough to follow his lead?

REFLECTION

God's ways are so different from yours. Where do you find this to be most true in your life? How does that challenge you? Ask God to fill your heart with his peace.

My Thoughts

After reflecting on this devotion and follow-up questions, here are my thoughts.

My Response

This is how I can apply the message to my life.

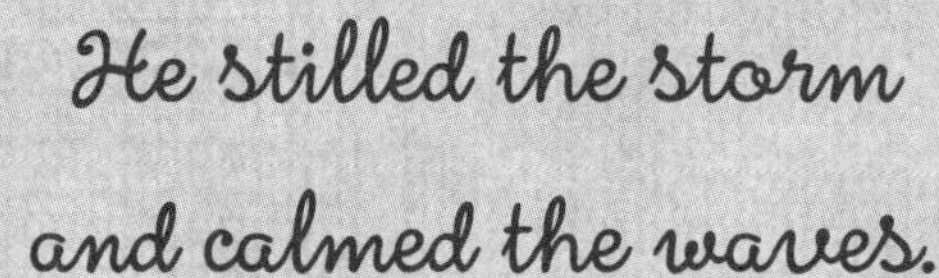

He stilled the storm and calmed the waves.

PSALM 107:29 NCV

To me, this Scripture feels most like (check one)

☐ A PROMISE ☐ AN INSTRUCTION ☐ A TRUTH

Here's how it impacts me...

PRAYER

GRATITUDE

I have been blessed with so many good things.
Here is what I am particularly thankful for this week.

REQUESTS

After reading and reflecting, here is what I'm asking God for.

WEEK 13

WHAT YOU CAN HANDLE

"I still have many things to tell you, but you can't bear them now."

JOHN 16:12 CSB

God does not give us all the information we will need at once. It would be too much for us to handle. He does, however, give us wisdom and direction for each step. Do we trust that even though we can't see the future, he is with us and will to guide us?

Pursuing the Lord for answers is a wonderful and valuable quest. As we get to know God's character more, especially his faithfulness as he walks with us through the hills and the valleys of this life, we learn to trust that what he offers is enough for the present moment. There is more than enough grace. There is love that overwhelmingly sustains us. He gives us what we need, so let's not get ahead of ourselves worrying about the future.

REFLECTION

Do you feel like you need all the answers now? How can you stay grounded in God's love, so your attention is on his gracious provision and wisdom instead?

My Thoughts

After reflecting on this devotion and follow-up questions, here are my thoughts.

My Response

This is how I can apply the message to my life.

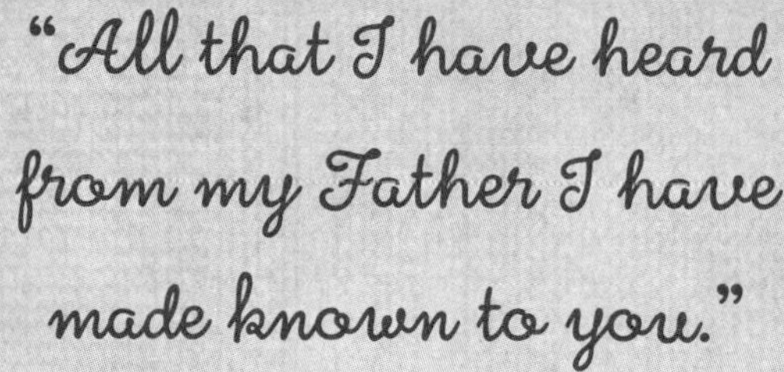

"All that I have heard from my Father I have made known to you."

JOHN 15:15 ESV

To me, this Scripture feels most like (check one)

☐ A PROMISE ☐ AN INSTRUCTION ☐ A TRUTH

Here's how it impacts me...

PRAYER

GRATITUDE

I have been blessed with so many good things.
Here is what I am particularly thankful for this week.

REQUESTS

After reading and reflecting, here is what I'm asking God for.

WEEK 14

PROPER PERSPECTIVE

Jesus said, "If you were blind, you would not be guilty of sin. But since you keep saying you see, your guilt remains."

JOHN 9:41 NCV

When we are young, we can't grasp the understanding adults have. In the same way, when we are innocent in our limited perspectives, we can only do better when we know better. With maturity, we see through hindsight what we didn't know at the time. It teaches us to loosen our grasp on what we feel is certain right now; it may change with further time, experience, and perspective.

God will not despise a humble heart. Why? Because it is teachable. It can admit when and where it is wrong, seek forgiveness and restoration, and make necessary changes with new information. We must keep estimations of ourselves grounded in the reality that we are still learning. Then, Jesus can direct our yielded hearts in his love and truth.

REFLECTION

Humble yourself before God. Thank him for receiving you whenever you go to him. What wrong perspectives may have gotten in the way of you learning new things about God?

My Thoughts

After reflecting on this devotion and follow-up questions, here are my thoughts.

My Response

This is how I can apply the message to my life.

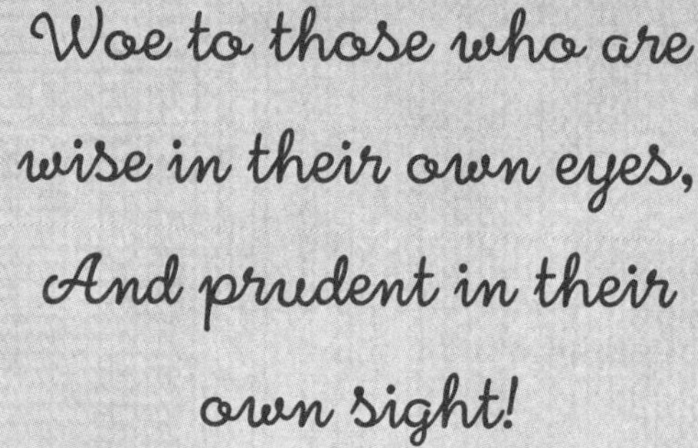

Woe to those who are
wise in their own eyes,
And prudent in their
own sight!

ISAIAH 5:21 NKJV

To me, this Scripture feels most like (check one)

☐ A PROMISE ☐ AN INSTRUCTION ☐ A TRUTH

Here's how it impacts me…

PRAYER

GRATITUDE

I have been blessed with so many good things.
Here is what I am particularly thankful for this week.

REQUESTS

After reading and reflecting, here is what I'm asking God for.

WEEK 15

QUIET GIVING

> "When you give to the poor, don't be like the hypocrites. They blow trumpets in the synagogues and on the streets so that people will see them and honor them. I tell you the truth, those hypocrites already have their full reward."
>
> MATTHEW 6:2 NCV

Generosity is one of the core values of God's kingdom. If we want to be like Jesus, we can't ignore the importance of giving to others. There is always a return on gifts we give, but Jesus reminds us to wait on God for our true reward. Out of a heart of love, we can give to the Lord and others and not for praise from those who know what we are doing.

In fact, Jesus takes it even a step further when he says, "when you give to the poor, don't let anyone know what you are doing" (Matthew 6:3). When you give to the poor, Jesus says, not if. Do we make giving to the poor a priority by building it into our budgets? If not, now is the time to set it up. Do it quietly unto the Lord; it is an act of worship and stewardship.

REFLECTION

How can you be more generous with your resources and give with a heart of love?

My Thoughts

After reflecting on this devotion and follow-up questions, here are my thoughts.

My Response

This is how I can apply the message to my life.

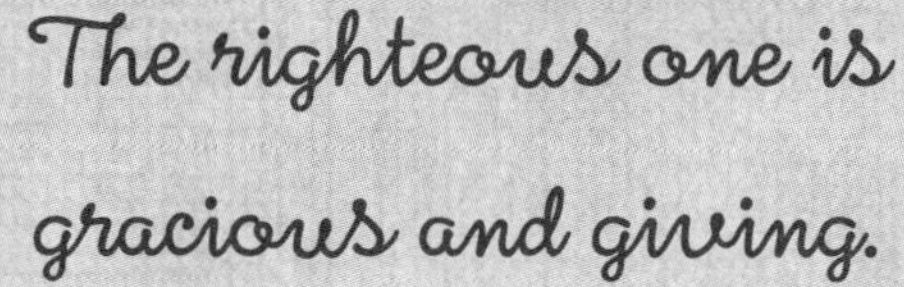

The righteous one is gracious and giving.

PSALM 37:21 CSB

To me, this Scripture feels most like (check one)

☐ A PROMISE ☐ AN INSTRUCTION ☐ A TRUTH

Here's how it impacts me...

PRAYER

GRATITUDE

I have been blessed with so many good things.
Here is what I am particularly thankful for this week.

REQUESTS

After reading and reflecting, here is what I'm asking God for.

WEEK 16

UNDERSTANDABLE TERMS

> Then He said to them, "Follow Me, and I will make you fishers of men."
>
> MATTHEW 4:19 NKJV

Jesus met each of his disciples where they were, and he called them in ways that built on their experience. Simon Peter, Andrew, Jacob, and John were all fishermen. Jesus called them to follow him and fish for men. Though it may sound funny to our ears, it must have been a captivating offer for these men to leave their livelihoods behind to follow him.

Just as Jesus spoke their language, he speaks yours. He knows the language of your heart and the experience and skills you have, and he calls you to follow him. Have you experienced the Lord enlightening and drawing your heart to him by speaking to you personally? His Spirit is with you to open your ears, bring understanding, and draw you closer to him as he teaches you the ways of his kingdom.

REFLECTION

Are you ready for God to call on you? Is your heart open to hearing from him? What is the language of your heart?

My Thoughts

After reflecting on this devotion and follow-up questions, here are my thoughts.

My Response

This is how I can apply the message to my life.

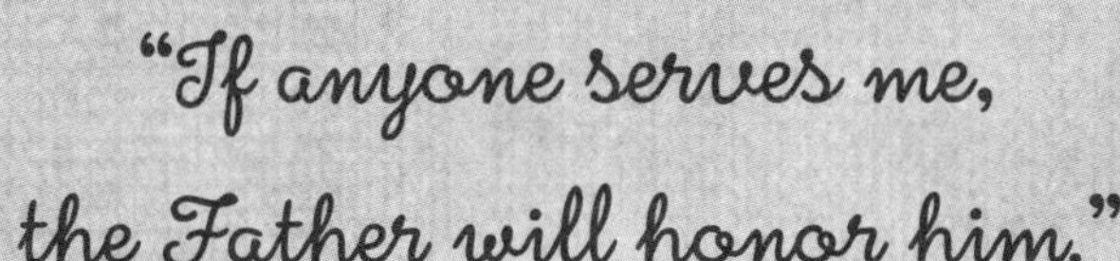

"If anyone serves me,
the Father will honor him."

JOHN 12:26 CSB

To me, this Scripture feels most like (check one)

☐ A PROMISE ☐ AN INSTRUCTION ☐ A TRUTH

Here's how it impacts me…

PRAYER

GRATITUDE

I have been blessed with so many good things.
Here is what I am particularly thankful for this week.

REQUESTS

After reading and reflecting, here is what I'm asking God for.

WEEK 17

RESIST OFFENSE

> "A prophet is honored everywhere except in his hometown and with his own people and in his own home."
>
> MARK 6:4 NCV

Keeping the heart open to hope and change is an important element of faith. We may resist the changes we see in others if we have known them well and for a long time. Our set expectations of them can be at odds with the people they are transforming into. This can be hard to overcome, but it's possible.

The people of Jesus' hometown resisted his message because they took offense at his confidence and message. They had watched him grow up. They had reasons why they thought the Messiah would not look so ordinary. Still, they had the same opportunity as other towns to witness the power of God work through him. Offense can cloud our faith, so we must hold on to the tension of natural realities and the mystery of God's mercy at the same time.

REFLECTION

Jesus healed diseases, caused blind eyes to see, and led a generation to the Father's heart. How have you kept him in a limited box based on your own experiences and expectations? How can you protect against offense?

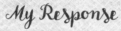

My Thoughts

After reflecting on this devotion and follow-up questions, here are my thoughts.

My Response

This is how I can apply the message to my life.

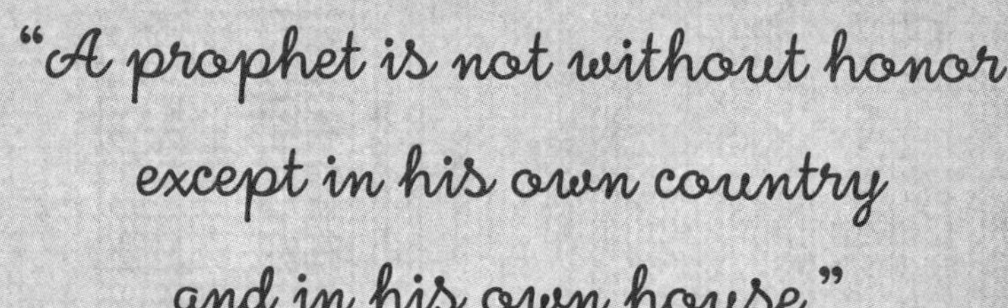

"A prophet is not without honor
except in his own country
and in his own house."

MATTHEW 13:57 NKJV

To me, this Scripture feels most like (check one)

☐ A PROMISE ☐ AN INSTRUCTION ☐ A TRUTH

Here's how it impacts me...

PRAYER

GRATITUDE

I have been blessed with so many good things.
Here is what I am particularly thankful for this week.

REQUESTS

After reading and reflecting, here is what I'm asking God for.

WEEK 18

COMPELLED BY COMPASSION

"I have compassion on the crowd, because they've already stayed with me three days and have nothing to eat."

MARK 8:2 CSB

Before Jesus performed the miracle of feeding thousands, he felt compassion for them. This compassion compelled him to act. They had come to hear Jesus speak about the kingdom of heaven and their loving Father, and Jesus could demonstrate the love and care of the Father by feeding them.

How often do we act out of obligation rather than compassion? What if we left room in our hearts for love to move us? Jesus had spent three days teaching thousands of people, and they had nothing to eat. He showed both the power of God and the kindness of his mercy by blessing what food there was and having the disciples distribute it. After the people had been miraculously fed, he sent them on their way. Before you go on your way, let the compassion of Christ meet you to satisfy your hunger and ready you for what's ahead.

REFLECTION

Jesus was moved by compassion to feed those who followed him. Ask him to meet your needs with the love of his presence. How can you rely on him and follow in his footsteps?

My Thoughts

After reflecting on this devotion and follow-up questions, here are my thoughts.

My Response

This is how I can apply the message to my life.

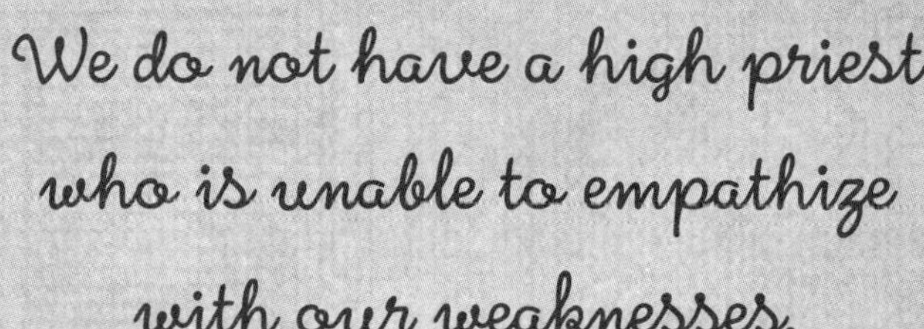

We do not have a high priest
who is unable to empathize
with our weaknesses.

HEBREWS 4:15 NIV

To me, this Scripture feels most like (check one)

☐ A PROMISE ☐ AN INSTRUCTION ☐ A TRUTH

Here's how it impacts me...

PRAYER

GRATITUDE

I have been blessed with so many good things.
Here is what I am particularly thankful for this week.

REQUESTS

After reading and reflecting, here is what I'm asking God for.

WEEK 19

CONNECTION TO THE FATHER

> "This is the way to have eternal life—to know you, the only true God, and Jesus Christ, the one you sent to earth."
>
> JOHN 17:3 NLT

In prayer, Jesus took the time to mention the beauty and power of knowing and experiencing God. Not only is it a joy and a gift; it's the way to eternal life. Having a deep understanding, a true relationship with God the Father and Jesus Christ the Son, is the power of God's life within us.

How important is personal connection to God to your faith? How well do you know Jesus? There is always more to discover, greater revelation to reach, and deeper fellowship to cultivate. With the help of the Holy Spirit, you can prioritize your relationship with God and listen to him, learn from his Word, and offer him access to your heart. As we do, he will correct us with kindness, break through our limits with his love, and instruct us in his perfect wisdom.

REFLECTION

What do you believe was the deepest reason Jesus came to the earth? How will you pursue knowing him more?

My Thoughts

After reflecting on this devotion and follow-up questions, here are my thoughts.

My Response

This is how I can apply the message to my life.

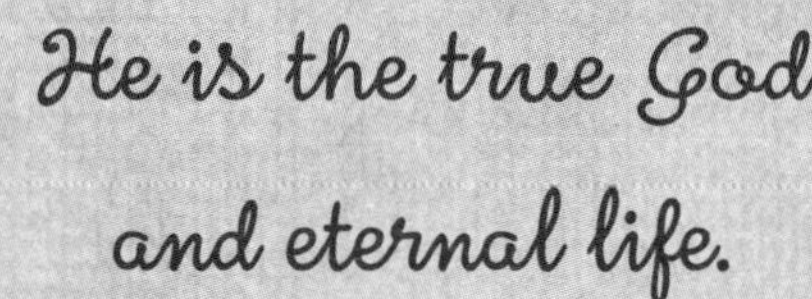

He is the true God
and eternal life.

1 JOHN 5:20 NIV

To me, this Scripture feels most like (check one)

☐ A PROMISE ☐ AN INSTRUCTION ☐ A TRUTH

Here's how it impacts me...

PRAYER

GRATITUDE

I have been blessed with so many good things.
Here is what I am particularly thankful for this week.

REQUESTS

After reading and reflecting, here is what I'm asking God for.

WEEK 20

SAY WHAT YOU MEAN

> "Say only yes if you mean yes, and no if you mean no. If you say more than yes or no, it is from the Evil One."
>
> MATTHEW 5:37 NCV

There is power in honesty. When we say what we mean and follow through on what we say, nothing can trap us. We don't need to appease others with what we think they want to hear. It's more honorable to be true to our word.

Jesus knew the power of a promise, and he did not condone making a vow lightly. His kindness instructs us to be clear with our communication. It is a loving act, both for us and others, when we are clear about what we can and can't do. Embrace the beauty of clarity even if it means disappointing others. It would be greater trouble to say something we don't mean and not follow through on it later.

REFLECTION

All the teachings of Jesus are based in kindness, goodness, and truth. Instead of writing off the wisdom of his Word, live by it. How can you be clear and thoughtful in your communication and commitment?

My Thoughts

After reflecting on this devotion and follow-up questions, here are my thoughts.

My Response

This is how I can apply the message to my life.

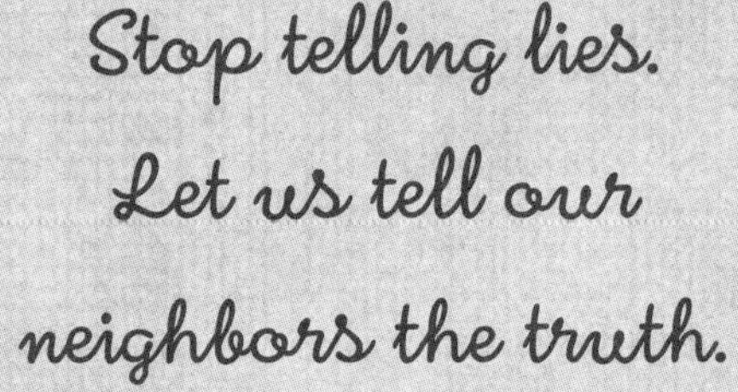

Stop telling lies.
Let us tell our
neighbors the truth.

EPHESIANS 4:25 NLT

To me, this Scripture feels most like (check one)

☐ A PROMISE ☐ AN INSTRUCTION ☐ A TRUTH

Here's how it impacts me...

PRAYER

GRATITUDE

I have been blessed with so many good things.
Here is what I am particularly thankful for this week.

REQUESTS

After reading and reflecting, here is what I'm asking God for.

WEEK 21

AMONG THE LIVING

> "Your mistake is that you don't know the Scriptures, and you don't know the power of God. He is the God of the living, not the dead. You have made a serious error."
>
> MARK 12:24, 27 NLT

What good is religion if it is for the dead but not the living? The hope of eternal life is wonderful, but what about the transformative power of God's life within us now? If all we have to look forward to is death, where is the joy of God's promises? Where is the peace of his presence? Where is the comfort of his love?

We need a God who is with us now, and he is. He promises to never leave or forsake those who look to him. He promises to strengthen, uphold, heal, and comfort the needy when they call on him. We need a faith rooted in our lived reality and not just the promise of a better reality to come. We need both. The revelation of the Scriptures and the power of God are for us to experience here and now, and they bring hope for what is to come.

REFLECTION

How do you know the power of Jesus' life in your own? Don't just scrape by each day. Give your heart completely to God. Ask him to fill it with the revelation of his power.

My Thoughts

After reflecting on this devotion and follow-up questions, here are my thoughts.

My Response

This is how I can apply the message to my life.

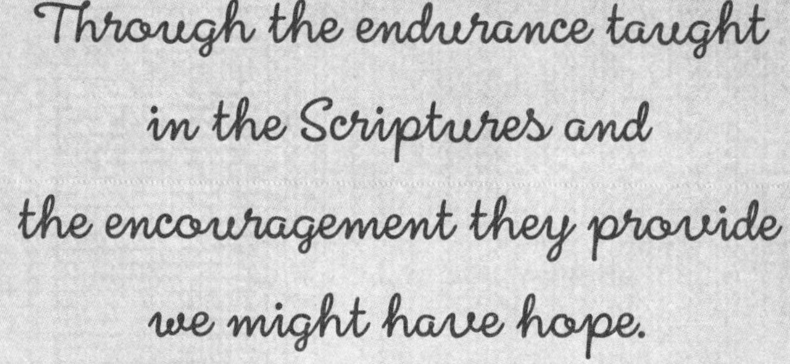

Through the endurance taught
in the Scriptures and
the encouragement they provide
we might have hope.

ROMANS 15:4 NIV

To me, this Scripture feels most like (check one)

☐ A PROMISE ☐ AN INSTRUCTION ☐ A TRUTH

Here's how it impacts me...

PRAYER

GRATITUDE

I have been blessed with so many good things.
Here is what I am particularly thankful for this week.

REQUESTS

After reading and reflecting, here is what I'm asking God for.

WEEK 22

PROMOTED BY GOD

"Everyone who exalts himself will be humbled, and the one who humbles himself will be exalted."

LUKE 14:11 NASB

When we remain humble before God and others, we slow down when others may tend to overwork to draw attention to themselves. God sees what we do both in private and in public, and every bit of it counts. It is better that God promote us instead of trying to prove ourselves to others.

What is ours to focus on if not self-promotion or proving ourselves? It is to do with integrity the work given to us. Treat others the way you want to be treated. Be kind, follow through on your word, and pursue peace. Let your lifestyle be one no one can argue with, for you have nothing to hide when you walk in the light of Christ's kingdom. Let love lead and keep grace flowing. It is human to err, but it is godly to extend mercy.

REFLECTION

How can you keep from striving for your place in this world and fighting for attention? Stand in the confidence of who God says you are. How will you live humbly before God and others?

My Thoughts

After reflecting on this devotion and follow-up questions, here are my thoughts.

My Response

This is how I can apply the message to my life.

Pride ends in humiliation,
while humility brings honor.

PROVERBS 29:23 NLT

To me, this Scripture feels most like (check one)

☐ A PROMISE ☐ AN INSTRUCTION ☐ A TRUTH

Here's how it impacts me...

PRAYER

GRATITUDE

I have been blessed with so many good things.
Here is what I am particularly thankful for this week.

REQUESTS

After reading and reflecting, here is what I'm asking God for.

WEEK 23

DISTRACTING DETAILS

"Why all this fussing over forgetting to bring bread? Do you still not see or understand what I say to you? Are your hearts still hard?"

MARK 8:17 TPT

The disciples were confused by Jesus' warning in an earlier verse to be on their guard against the yeast of the Pharisees. They thought he was chastising them for not bringing bread. How often we misunderstand the words of Jesus! Still, he is kind and patient with us. He teaches us so we will grow in our understanding. Even as he corrects the disciples, he has the heart of a teacher.

Instead of jumping to conclusions in our confusion, we can ask the Lord for clarification. He brings perspective to our cloudy thoughts. We don't always read him right, and it's important to recognize this so we remain humble and teachable. Soften your heart to the Lord and his voice. Listen to understand and not just hear. His wisdom enlightens hearts, and his Spirit brings revelation to minds.

REFLECTION

How can you guard against getting caught up in details that don't matter? What does it look like to open the ears of your heart so you can know God more?

My Thoughts

After reflecting on this devotion and follow-up questions, here are my thoughts.

My Response

This is how I can apply the message to my life.

"We can see that you know all things and that you do not even need to have anyone ask you questions."

JOHN 16:30 NIV

To me, this Scripture feels most like (check one)

☐ A PROMISE ☐ AN INSTRUCTION ☐ A TRUTH

Here's how it impacts me...

PRAYER

GRATITUDE

I have been blessed with so many good things.
Here is what I am particularly thankful for this week.

REQUESTS

After reading and reflecting, here is what I'm asking God for.

WEEK 24

COME AND REST

"Come aside by yourselves to a deserted place and rest a while." For there were many coming and going, and they did not even have time to eat.

MARK 6:31 NKJV

Has the pace of life drained you? There are always more tasks than there is time. Jesus doesn't expect you to burn out while serving others. He invites you to come to a place where there are no demands. He invites you to rest with him.

Do you resist taking time for yourself? Do you prioritize the needs of others so much that you neglect your own? You need nourishment, rest, and play as much as anyone else. You don't have to prove your love by neglecting yourself. That is a sure way to resentment and exhaustion. Take time to rest. Don't let the *shoulds* of life or the unending needs of others keep you from taking the time necessary to refresh and regroup. Take Jesus' offer and come aside by yourself to a deserted place and rest awhile.

REFLECTION

Thank God for loving you well. Rest is not a luxury but a necessity. How will you take time to rest instead of overworking?

My Thoughts

After reflecting on this devotion and follow-up questions, here are my thoughts.

My Response

This is how I can apply the message to my life.

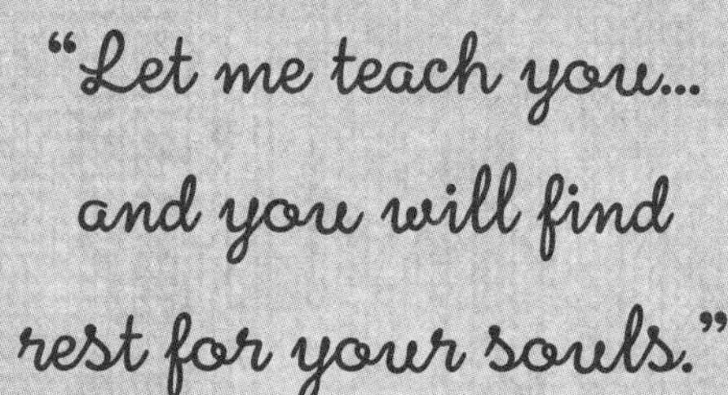

"Let me teach you...
and you will find
rest for your souls."

MATTHEW 11:29 NLT

To me, this Scripture feels most like (check one)

☐ A PROMISE ☐ AN INSTRUCTION ☐ A TRUTH

Here's how it impacts me...

PRAYER

GRATITUDE

I have been blessed with so many good things.
Here is what I am particularly thankful for this week.

REQUESTS

After reading and reflecting, here is what I'm asking God for.

WEEK 25

EMBRACED BY LOVE

"Those the Father has given me will come to me, and I will never reject them."

JOHN 6:37 NLT

Jesus promises he will never turn away someone who comes to him. When we believe in Christ the Son and turn to him for wisdom, direction, and our identity as children of God, we are embraced by love. Does this mean we come to him perfectly? No. He perfects us by covering us in his gracious mercy. In him, we are made whole.

Have you been keeping your distance from Jesus? Do you hesitate to come to him? Do your questions, doubts, or longings make you feel as if you don't deserve his love? Nothing can separate you from his mercy, so don't let your excuses keep you away. He is standing with open arms ready to embrace you as you are.

REFLECTION

Thank God for not requiring perfection from you. How can you quiet the questions, doubts, and longings that make you feel like you don't deserve his love? Don't stay away from him today. Let him wrap you in his love.

My Thoughts

After reflecting on this devotion and follow-up questions, here are my thoughts.

My Response

This is how I can apply the message to my life.

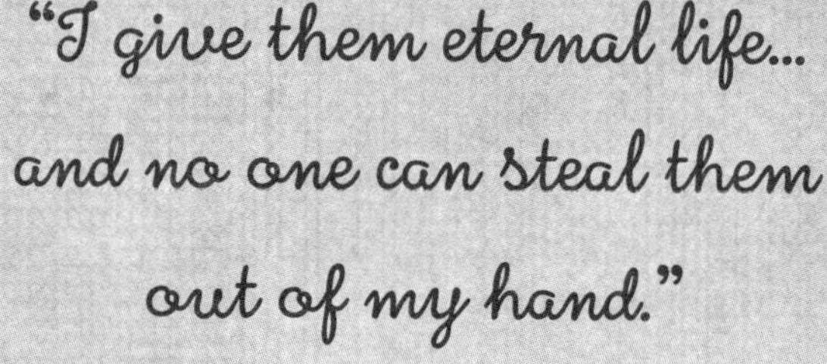

*"I give them eternal life...
and no one can steal them
out of my hand."*

JOHN 10:28 NCV

To me, this Scripture feels most like (check one)

☐ A PROMISE ☐ AN INSTRUCTION ☐ A TRUTH

Here's how it impacts me...

PRAYER

GRATITUDE

I have been blessed with so many good things.
Here is what I am particularly thankful for this week.

REQUESTS

After reading and reflecting, here is what I'm asking God for.

WEEK 26

LAY IT DOWN

> Calling the crowd along with his disciples, he said to them, "If anyone wants to follow after me, let him deny himself, take up his cross, and follow me."
>
> MARK 8:34 CSB

Surrender is necessary to follow Christ. We must be willing to give up habits, preferences, and judgments. We need to let go of those chips on our shoulders to forgive and move toward mercy instead of away from it. This path of love that Christ calls us on isn't the easiest path to follow, but it's worth it.

Have we really laid down our rights to our comfort and getting even? Have we truly surrendered to Jesus' leadership? If we have, our hearts remain humble and open. We allow the teachings and example of Christ to transform us and challenge us. We can't stay the same when we follow him. Lay down your resistance, and let his love lead you. No matter how hard it gets, he will not leave you.

REFLECTION

How do you lay down your life and follow Christ? In what ways do you surrender and give up your hold on comfort? Do you trust that God knows better than you do?

My Thoughts

After reflecting on this devotion and follow-up questions, here are my thoughts.

My Response

This is how I can apply the message to my life.

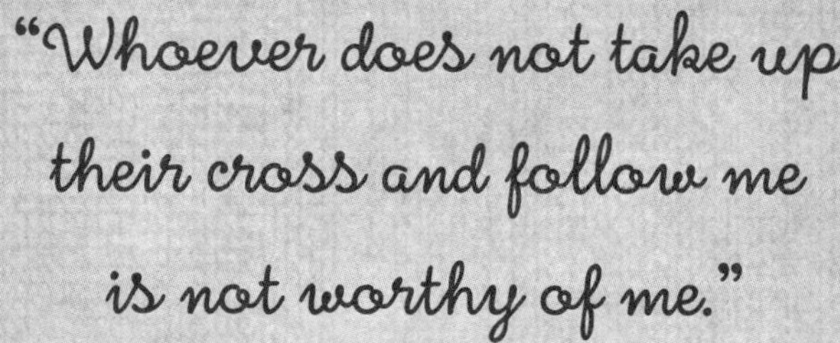

"Whoever does not take up
their cross and follow me
is not worthy of me."

MATTHEW 10:38 NIV

To me, this Scripture feels most like (check one)

☐ A PROMISE ☐ AN INSTRUCTION ☐ A TRUTH

Here's how it impacts me…

PRAYER

GRATITUDE

I have been blessed with so many good things.
Here is what I am particularly thankful for this week.

REQUESTS

After reading and reflecting, here is what I'm asking God for.

WEEK 27

CHECK YOUR HEART

> "You are those who justify yourselves before men, but God knows your hearts. For what is highly esteemed among men is an abomination in the sight of God."
>
> LUKE 16:15 NKJV

It does not matter how spiritual we appear to others if our hearts are not submitted to God. If we hurl judgments at others in the name of God, we may seem very religious, but we are missing the point altogether. God leads in mercy, and we follow his lead.

It's important to be aware of our hearts. When we check in with the motivations behind why we say, think, feel, and do certain things, we have the opportunity to change. If we assume our motivations are pure, we may be fooling ourselves. We unconsciously pick up and assign meaning and attributes to God that aren't based in his character or Word. May we remain humble and teachable: ready to change course, admit when we are wrong, and ask for forgiveness.

REFLECTION

God's opinion of you should matter the most. He is the one who sees, knows, and judges rightly. How can you leave that job to him? How do you feel transformed in the power of his mercy?

My Thoughts

After reflecting on this devotion and follow-up questions, here are my thoughts.

My Response

This is how I can apply the message to my life.

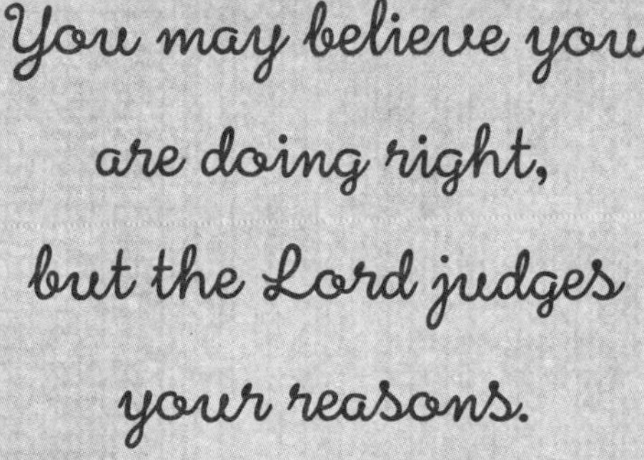

You may believe you
are doing right,
but the Lord judges
your reasons.

PROVERBS 21:2 NCV

To me, this Scripture feels most like (check one)

☐ A PROMISE ☐ AN INSTRUCTION ☐ A TRUTH

Here's how it impacts me...

PRAYER

GRATITUDE

I have been blessed with so many good things.
Here is what I am particularly thankful for this week.

REQUESTS

After reading and reflecting, here is what I'm asking God for.

WEEK 28

GRACE IN THE WORLD

"I am not asking You to take them out of the world, but to keep them away from the evil one."

JOHN 17:15 NASB

We are not called to live secluded from the world. There is no reason to build communes or kingdoms of our own making. We are in the world to live, work, and relate to all types of people. Our hearts can stay pure in the love of Christ even while we interact with those who don't know him.

We can't be influential if we are removed from the world. We must take our places in the kingdom of God and in the spheres of influence we inhabit. We should not run from these things but embrace them. We do this by spending time with the Lord each day, inviting him to transform us, and allowing him to move through us as we live with integrity, purpose, and compassion.

REFLECTION

How do you join with the prayer of Jesus to the Father? In what ways does your love for others reflect his love for you?

My Thoughts

After reflecting on this devotion and follow-up questions, here are my thoughts.

My Response

This is how I can apply the message to my life.

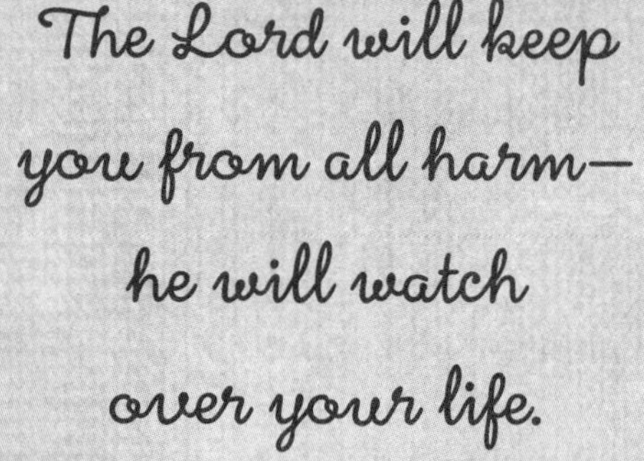

The Lord will keep
you from all harm—
he will watch
over your life.

PSALM 121:7 NIV

To me, this Scripture feels most like (check one)

☐ A PROMISE ☐ AN INSTRUCTION ☐ A TRUTH

Here's how it impacts me...

PRAYER

GRATITUDE

I have been blessed with so many good things.
Here is what I am particularly thankful for this week.

REQUESTS

After reading and reflecting, here is what I'm asking God for.

WEEK 29

SIGNIFICANT TO HIM

"Are not two sparrows sold for a penny? Yet not one of them will fall to the ground outside your Father's care."

MATTHEW 10:29 NIV

Nothing in this world escapes the notice of the Creator. Jesus said no sparrow falls to the ground without the Father's knowledge. If the Father cares for small birds that others don't pay attention to, how much more does he care for those he created in his image? We were made to reflect the nature of God.

Lay down your worries, big and small, about the details of your life. You don't have to ignore them; simply hand them over to Jesus. God knows what we need before we know to ask for it. We can trust his heart, power, and character to care for us when we are in need. Nothing is too insignificant for him.

REFLECTION

Go to God with all your worries including the small, seemingly insignificant things. Do you trust him more than you worry about the details of your life? How can you let go of the weight of worry and walk in the fullness of his liberating love?

My Thoughts

After reflecting on this devotion and follow-up questions, here are my thoughts.

My Response

This is how I can apply the message to my life.

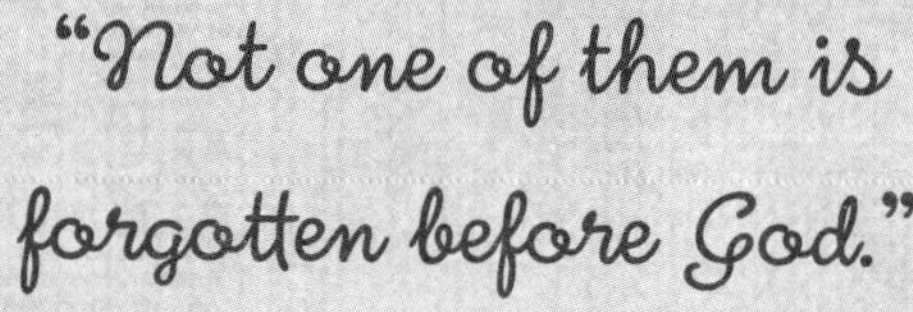

"Not one of them is forgotten before God."

LUKE 12:6 ESV

To me, this Scripture feels most like (check one)

☐ A PROMISE ☐ AN INSTRUCTION ☐ A TRUTH

Here's how it impacts me...

PRAYER

GRATITUDE

I have been blessed with so many good things.
Here is what I am particularly thankful for this week.

REQUESTS

After reading and reflecting, here is what I'm asking God for.

WEEK 30

OUR CENTER

"When you pray, say:
'Father, hallowed be your name.
Your kingdom come.'"

LUKE 11:2 ESV

When we set the glory of God's name at our center, we make his opinion the sun around which we orbit. His truth becomes our anchor. We are grounded by his nature, Word, and power. This is the beginning of Jesus' teaching on prayer; we center our lives, hearts, and attention around the glory of the Father.

Before we move on with the day, let's focus our hearts on this basic truth. The Father is full of glory, love, and power. His ways are truer, wiser, and kinder than the world's. We look first to him and allow his perspective and holiness to wash over us. Then, we join with his heart and ask his Spirit to wash over us and bring the reality of his kingdom to earth.

REFLECTION

Thank Jesus for giving you an example of how to pray. Is God at the center of your life? Who do you look to when things go wrong? Who do you ask for advice or help?

My Thoughts

After reflecting on this devotion and follow-up questions, here are my thoughts.

My Response

This is how I can apply the message to my life.

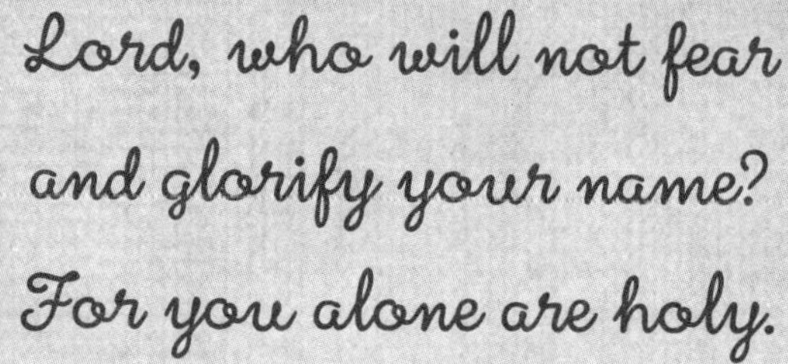

Lord, who will not fear
and glorify your name?
For you alone are holy.

REVELATION 15:4 CSB

To me, this Scripture feels most like (check one)

☐ A PROMISE ☐ AN INSTRUCTION ☐ A TRUTH

Here's how it impacts me…

PRAYER

GRATITUDE

I have been blessed with so many good things.
Here is what I am particularly thankful for this week.

REQUESTS

After reading and reflecting, here is what I'm asking God for.

WEEK 31

SPIRIT AND TRUTH

> "The time is coming when the true worshipers will worship the Father in spirit and truth, and that time is here already. You see, the Father too is actively seeking such people to worship him."
>
> JOHN 4:23 NCV

Worship is not defined by where we are geographically. It is not something that must be done through rites in a church, temple, or other designated sacred space. To worship God in spirit and in truth is to worship him with our lives and obey his Word. No matter where we are, we offer God the worship of our surrendered hearts.

Have you ever considered that mundane tasks, when done with an attitude of submission and love, can be an expression of worship? That turns doing the dishes, buying groceries, cooking meals, switching out the laundry, going on walks, and more into opportunities to worship the Lord in spirit and truth. We can intentionally turn our attention to the Lord throughout the day and offer him the surrender of our love.

REFLECTION

How do you worship God in spirit and in truth? Ask him to fill you with the power of his Spirit as you turn your heart to him in humble awe. How does he meet you in the mundane tasks of life?

My Thoughts

After reflecting on this devotion and follow-up questions, here are my thoughts.

My Response

This is how I can apply the message to my life.

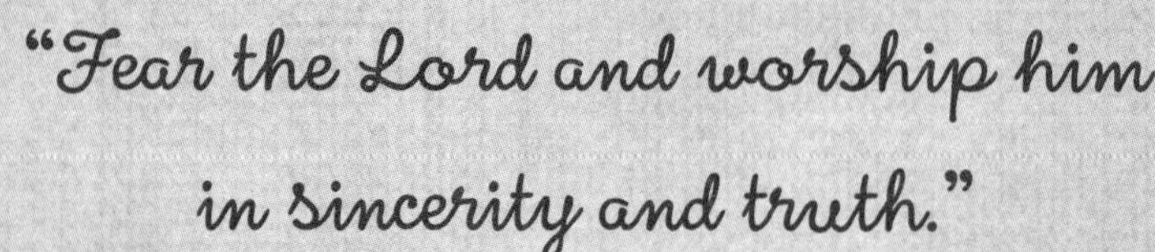

"Fear the Lord and worship him in sincerity and truth."

JOSHUA 24:14 CSB

To me, this Scripture feels most like (check one)

☐ A PROMISE ☐ AN INSTRUCTION ☐ A TRUTH

Here's how it impacts me...

PRAYER

GRATITUDE

I have been blessed with so many good things.
Here is what I am particularly thankful for this week.

REQUESTS

After reading and reflecting, here is what I'm asking God for.

WEEK 32

LOVING OBEDIENCE

"You are my friends if you do what I command you."

JOHN 15:14 ESV

Obedience to Jesus' words and teachings reflects our relationship to him. If we trust Jesus is the Son of God, revealing the heart of the Father, why would we ignore his directions? He is the wisdom of God in human form; he experienced everything we go through. If he isn't trustworthy, who is?

Jesus called his disciples friends and not servants. He gave them direction, but he also taught them what the Father had revealed. Servants don't always understand their employer, but Jesus shared with his friends what the Father was doing. He still calls us friends, and he gives his Spirit to bring power and perspective to our lives. We offer him our obedience in return.

REFLECTION

Thank Jesus for sharing the heart of the Father and not just giving rules and regulations without explanation. How do you honor Jesus as your friend?

My Thoughts

After reflecting on this devotion and follow-up questions, here are my thoughts.

My Response

This is how I can apply the message to my life.

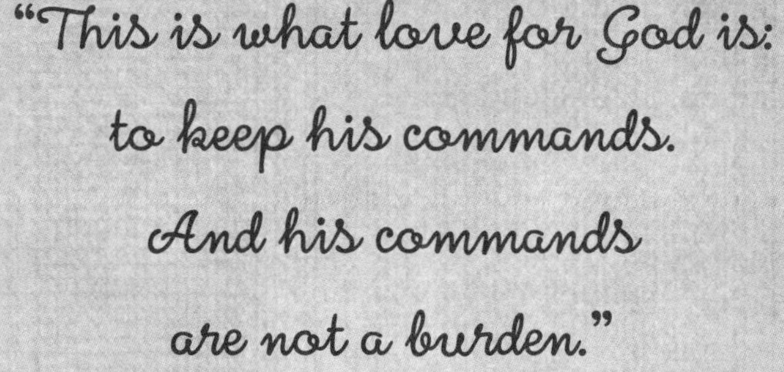

"This is what love for God is:
to keep his commands.
And his commands
are not a burden."

1 JOHN 5:3 CSB

To me, this Scripture feels most like (check one)

☐ A PROMISE ☐ AN INSTRUCTION ☐ A TRUTH

Here's how it impacts me…

PRAYER

GRATITUDE

I have been blessed with so many good things.
Here is what I am particularly thankful for this week.

REQUESTS

After reading and reflecting, here is what I'm asking God for.

WEEK 33

COURAGE TO SPEAK

> One night the Lord spoke to Paul in a vision and told him, "Don't be afraid! Speak out! Don't be silent! For I am with you, and no one will attack and harm you, for many people in this city belong to me."
>
> ACTS 18:9-10 NLT

Sometimes direct encouragement from the Lord is exactly what we need. The reassurance that God's presence will never leave us, and he will give us right words to say, is a relief. When God calls us to something, he equips us, and he promises to be with us through it all.

Receive the words of Christ in your present season. Reread the verse for today through the lens of Jesus speaking directly to you. He is with you; have no fear. He will give you the words you need at the right moment. Don't be intimidated by others, for the powerful presence of God is at work within and through you. Invite the Spirit to minister directly to your heart as you receive the kindness of Jesus through his Word.

REFLECTION

God has promised to never leave you. Ask for courage to continue in the way that he has called you. What words has he spoken to you that you continue to draw encouragement from?

My Thoughts

After reflecting on this devotion and follow-up questions, here are my thoughts.

My Response

This is how I can apply the message to my life.

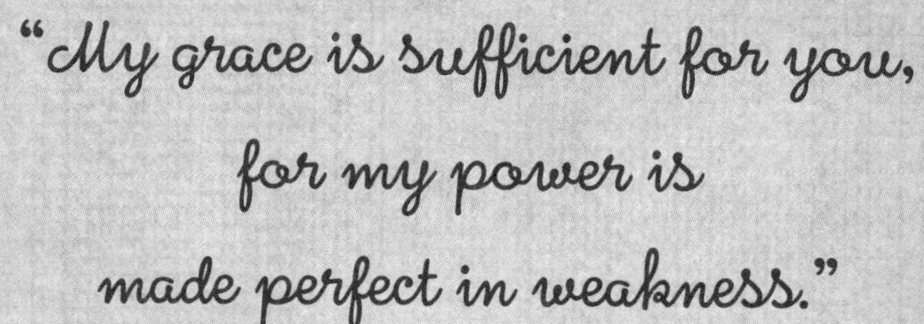

"My grace is sufficient for you,
for my power is
made perfect in weakness."

2 CORINTHIANS 12:9 NIV

To me, this Scripture feels most like (check one)

☐ A PROMISE ☐ AN INSTRUCTION ☐ A TRUTH

Here's how it impacts me...

PRAYER

GRATITUDE

I have been blessed with so many good things.
Here is what I am particularly thankful for this week.

REQUESTS

After reading and reflecting, here is what I'm asking God for.

WEEK 34

BEGINNING AND END

When I saw him, I fell at his feet as if I were dead. But he laid his right hand on me and said, "Don't be afraid! I am the First and the Last."

REVELATION 1:17 NLT

Jesus is the first and last, the beginning and the end. He was there in the beginning, and he will be through every generation. There is no time and space where he is not. It's hard to wrap our heads around, but it's true. With this reality in mind, let's meditate on his relentless presence that does not leave or waver.

The love of God is his very nature. Where the Lord is, there is overflowing mercy. Instead of letting fear push us to self-protect or lash out, we can grab hold of the peace of Christ that settles our fears and gives us courage to walk with him. He never changes, and he never will. He is the same from age to age. He can't be contained by people's misgivings or misunderstandings of his character. He is powerfully persistent in merciful kindness, and his throne is built on righteous truth.

REFLECTION

How do you keep from judging God by the changing opinions in this world? In what ways is he your foundation, standard, and goal?

My Thoughts

After reflecting on this devotion and follow-up questions, here are my thoughts.

My Response

This is how I can apply the message to my life.

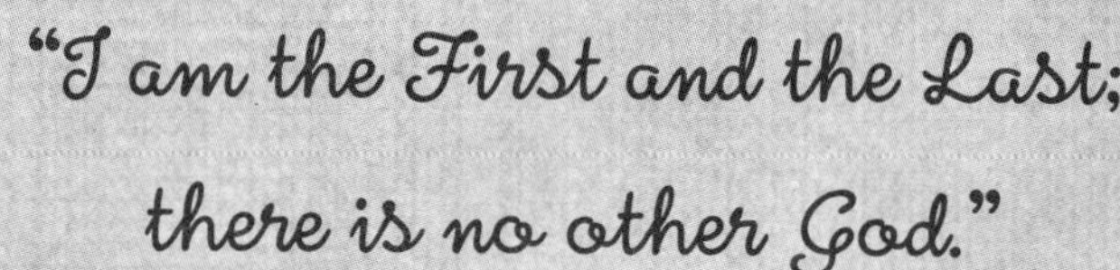

"I am the First and the Last;
there is no other God."

ISAIAH 44:6 NLT

To me, this Scripture feels most like (check one)

☐ A PROMISE ☐ AN INSTRUCTION ☐ A TRUTH

Here's how it impacts me...

PRAYER

GRATITUDE

I have been blessed with so many good things.
Here is what I am particularly thankful for this week.

REQUESTS

After reading and reflecting, here is what I'm asking God for.

WEEK 35

A GRIP TOO TIGHT

> "Whoever wants to save his life will lose it, but whoever loses his life for My sake and the gospel's will save it."
>
> MARK 8:35 NASB

To fully follow Jesus, we can't hold too tightly to our lives. Our resources are only ours for a short time. When we live in a mindset of generosity rather than scarcity, there is no reason to hold tightly. God has given us gifts; we can be generous with what we have been given.

What does it mean to choose to keep our lives for ourselves? Jesus answers this in the following verse (8:36): "For what does it benefit a person to gain the whole world, and forfeit his soul?" In other words, wealth and power mean nothing in the kingdom of God. While those with wealth and power can influence governments, economies, and cultures, they can't bribe the heart of God. The most important thing we can guard is our souls. How do we do this? By surrendering to the leadership of Christ no matter how much pride or position we need to sacrifice.

REFLECTION

The wisdom of God is better than the wisdom of the world. Why do you think God isn't impressed by prestige, power, or wealth? Have you surrendered your pride and position so your heart is wholly his?

My Thoughts

After reflecting on this devotion and follow-up questions, here are my thoughts.

My Response

This is how I can apply the message to my life.

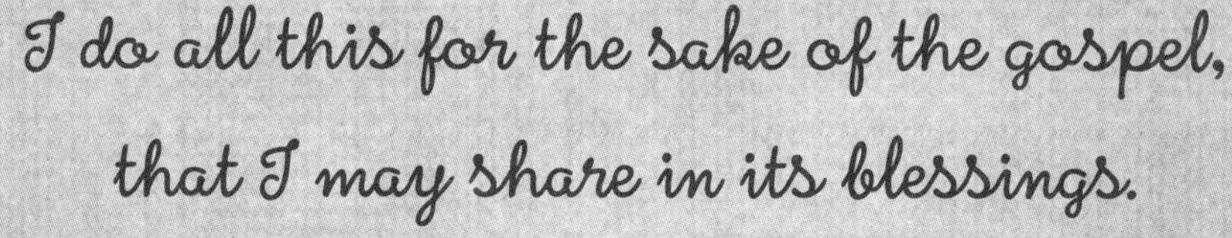

I do all this for the sake of the gospel, that I may share in its blessings.

1 CORINTHIANS 9:23 NIV

To me, this Scripture feels most like (check one)

☐ A PROMISE ☐ AN INSTRUCTION ☐ A TRUTH

Here's how it impacts me...

PRAYER

GRATITUDE

I have been blessed with so many good things.
Here is what I am particularly thankful for this week.

REQUESTS

After reading and reflecting, here is what I'm asking God for.

WEEK 36

NO EXCUSES

> "Love your enemies, and do good, and lend, expecting nothing in return, and your reward will be great, and you will be sons of the Most High, for he is kind to the ungrateful and the evil."
>
> LUKE 6:35 ESV

Where others put limits on their acts of generosity and love, Christ removed them all. Though a good person will give to a friend in need, who in their right mind would offer anything to an enemy? According to Christ, an enemy is as good as a friend when it comes to his love. There are no barriers to his merciful kindness.

We should pay attention to where we, or others, draw lines of distinction between who is worthy of our love and generosity and who is not. In the kingdom of Christ, every person receives the same measure. We are not exempt from showing love to those who offend, hate, or ridicule us; we are called to love them in the same way we love those closest to us. When we dare to be generous with compassion, we reflect the mercy of Christ.

REFLECTION

Is your generosity and love limited by your experiences? How do you break through the barriers of excuse and choose to love even those who have hurt you?

My Thoughts

After reflecting on this devotion and follow-up questions, here are my thoughts.

My Response

This is how I can apply the message to my life.

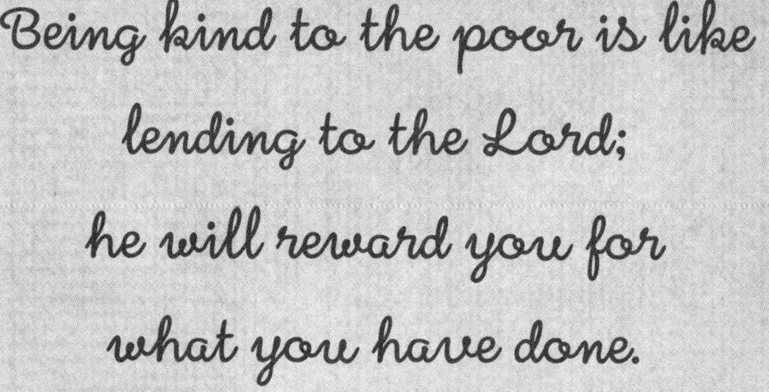

*Being kind to the poor is like
lending to the Lord;
he will reward you for
what you have done.*

PROVERBS 19:17 NCV

To me, this Scripture feels most like (check one)

☐ A PROMISE ☐ AN INSTRUCTION ☐ A TRUTH

Here's how it impacts me…

PRAYER

GRATITUDE

I have been blessed with so many good things.
Here is what I am particularly thankful for this week.

REQUESTS

After reading and reflecting, here is what I'm asking God for.

WEEK 37

WHAT MATTERS MOST

> "Why would you strive for food that is perishable and not be passionate to seek the food of eternal life, which never spoils? I, the Son of Man, am ready to give you what matters most, for God the Father has destined me for this purpose."
>
> JOHN 6:27 TPT

We can't live without food. In the same way, our souls need the nourishment of God's presence to flourish and grow. In today's verse, Jesus isn't saying we should give up working to meet our physical needs. He is saying that since we do work, how much more should we diligently seek the nourishment of God's kingdom that never spoils?

Jesus readily offers what matters most. He does this for each of us as we come to him. Do we take our spiritual hunger as seriously as our physical hunger? If we do, we will pursue the presence of Christ, obey his Word, and live in his law of love. As we do, we are fed and sustained by the life of God within us. There is more than enough to satisfy; keep feeding on his goodness.

REFLECTION

Thank God for his wonderful provision. How are you nourished by his Word? When do you find refreshment in his presence? In what ways do you feel satisfied by his love?

My Thoughts

After reflecting on this devotion and follow-up questions, here are my thoughts.

My Response

This is how I can apply the message to my life.

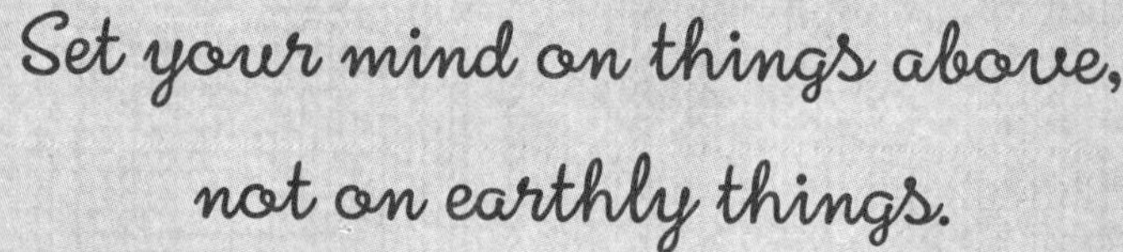

Set your mind on things above,
not on earthly things.

COLOSSIANS 3:2 NIV

To me, this Scripture feels most like (check one)

☐ A PROMISE ☐ AN INSTRUCTION ☐ A TRUTH

Here's how it impacts me…

PRAYER

GRATITUDE

I have been blessed with so many good things.
Here is what I am particularly thankful for this week.

REQUESTS

After reading and reflecting, here is what I'm asking God for.

WEEK 38

LIGHT OF THE WORLD

> "I am the light of the world. If you follow me, you won't have to walk in darkness, because you will have the light that leads to life."
>
> JOHN 8:12 NLT

Jesus' invitation to walk in the light of his life, wisdom, and love is as much for us as it was for the people he originally spoke to. His invitation is for all who come to him. We don't have to walk in darkness; Christ is the light that leads to life.

Whatever area of your life feels cloudy or confusing, bring it to Jesus and watch him light it up with his perfect presence. He gives peace that passes understanding, and even when our minds can't comprehend what he is doing, we can still experience the power of his love lighting up our hearts like a fire. Why hesitate to follow him?

REFLECTION

Thank God for meeting you with his powerful presence no matter where you are. What areas of your life feel cloudy or confusing? How can you trust him to guide you in those dark places?

My Thoughts

After reflecting on this devotion and follow-up questions, here are my thoughts.

My Response

This is how I can apply the message to my life.

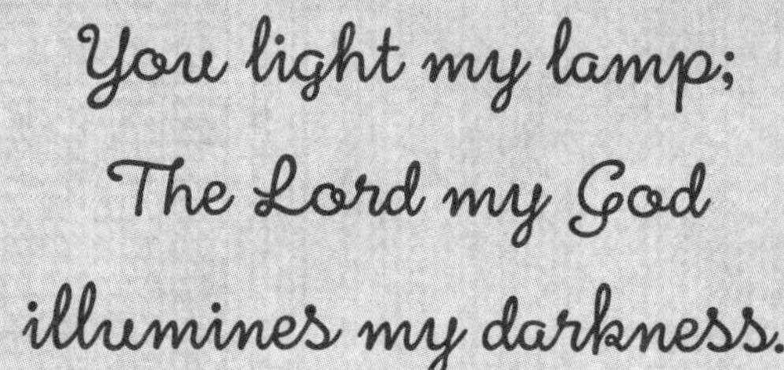

You light my lamp;
The Lord my God
illumines my darkness.

PSALM 18:28 NASB

To me, this Scripture feels most like (check one)

☐ A PROMISE ☐ AN INSTRUCTION ☐ A TRUTH

Here's how it impacts me...

PRAYER

GRATITUDE

I have been blessed with so many good things.
Here is what I am particularly thankful for this week.

REQUESTS

After reading and reflecting, here is what I'm asking God for.

WEEK 39

A LITTLE GOES FAR

"The kingdom of heaven is like yeast that a woman took and hid in a large tub of flour until it made all the dough rise."

MATTHEW 13:33 NCV

A little yeast is enough to affect a large amount of flour. A tiny light can infiltrate the darkness. A seed of faith can permeate a whole atmosphere. This is what Jesus says the kingdom of heaven is like; a little goes a long way.

We don't need perfect faith. We don't have to have it all figured out to follow the Lord. In fact, we can get overwhelmed by the big picture and lose sight of the practical steps needed to take to get there, if we are not careful. Instead of waiting until we have all the steps lined up, let's just take the steps we know to take today. Little things done with consistency and love will lead to big rewards.

REFLECTION

You don't have to have everything figured out to be obedient. What is your next small step? How can you consistently offer the little that you have?

My Thoughts

After reflecting on this devotion and follow-up questions, here are my thoughts.

My Response

This is how I can apply the message to my life.

The path of the righteous
is like the light of dawn,
which shines brighter and
brighter until full day.

PROVERBS 4:18 ESV

To me, this Scripture feels most like (check one)

☐ A PROMISE ☐ AN INSTRUCTION ☐ A TRUTH

Here's how it impacts me…

PRAYER

GRATITUDE

I have been blessed with so many good things.
Here is what I am particularly thankful for this week.

REQUESTS

After reading and reflecting, here is what I'm asking God for.

WEEK 40

EVEN MORE

"Whoever has, more will be given to him, and whoever does not have, even what he has will be taken away from him."

MARK 4:25 CSB

When we listen with open hearts to understand, we receive more revelation. If we remain closed off, however, what little we think we have will be lost. The truth of God is given to those who willingly receive it. Do we think we know all there is to know about God?

We need humility and curiosity to be open to teaching. Let us be like children who find joy in learning and growing. As we do, we will be given more, just as children are given more capacity to grow in their understanding as they delight in each new discovery and mastery of things once unattainable to them.

REFLECTION

Do you claim to know everything in any area? How does this affect your ability to receive? Ask God to increase your understanding as you delight in discovering more of his kingdom and his heart.

My Thoughts

After reflecting on this devotion and follow-up questions, here are my thoughts.

My Response

This is how I can apply the message to my life.

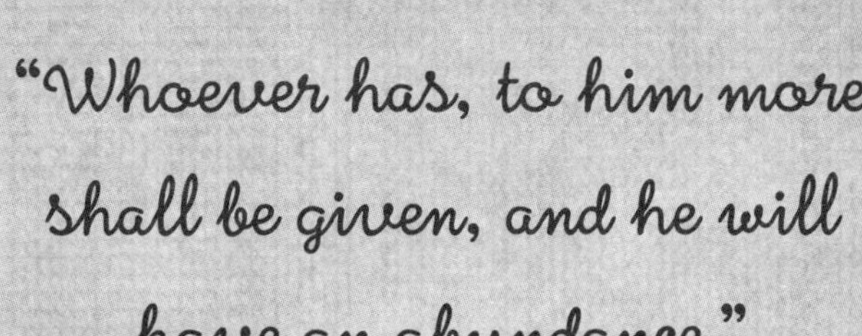

"Whoever has, to him more shall be given, and he will have an abundance."

MATTHEW 13:12 NASB

To me, this Scripture feels most like (check one)

☐ A PROMISE ☐ AN INSTRUCTION ☐ A TRUTH

Here's how it impacts me…

PRAYER

GRATITUDE

I have been blessed with so many good things.
Here is what I am particularly thankful for this week.

REQUESTS

After reading and reflecting, here is what I'm asking God for.

WEEK 41

PASSIONATE PURSUIT

> "If you want to test my teachings and discover where I received them, first be passionate to do God's will, and then you will be able to discern if my teachings are from the heart of God or from my own opinions."
>
> JOHN 7:17 TPT

Jesus was strategic when he told those who wanted to test his teachings that they must first be passionate to do God's will. Anyone can critique or criticize without surrendering to God or serving him. If we are not invested in finding solutions, our judgments are biased, and our hearts may remain closed off to understanding.

Passionate pursuit of God and his ways is the first step to truly knowing him. If we stay at a distance and only go to him when it's convenient, we miss out on much of what God has to offer. If we truly know the Lord, we understand his character and learn what his voice sounds like and what his presence feels like. Before we claim to know better, we must know the one who holds all wisdom.

REFLECTION

Thank God for sharing his wisdom with you. How can you lay down your preconceived notions about God, and pursue him passionately? How do you align your life with his ways?

My Thoughts

After reflecting on this devotion and follow-up questions, here are my thoughts.

My Response

This is how I can apply the message to my life.

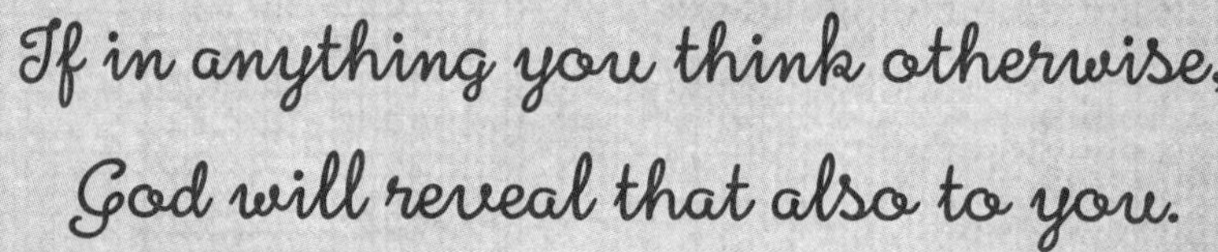

If in anything you think otherwise, God will reveal that also to you.

PHILIPPIANS 3:15 ESV

To me, this Scripture feels most like (check one)

☐ A PROMISE ☐ AN INSTRUCTION ☐ A TRUTH

Here's how it impacts me...

PRAYER

GRATITUDE

I have been blessed with so many good things.
Here is what I am particularly thankful for this week.

REQUESTS

After reading and reflecting, here is what I'm asking God for.

WEEK 42

ABUNDANT GROWTH

"The Kingdom of Heaven is like a mustard seed planted in a field. It is the smallest of all seeds, but it becomes the largest of garden plants; it grows into a tree, and birds come and make nests in its branches."

MATTHEW 13:31-32 NLT

The kingdom of heaven is planted like a small seed in our hearts, and when we allow it to take root within us, it grows exponentially. When we nurture the word of Christ, submitting to his leadership and following his ways, the kingdom expands in us.

The kingdom of Christ is more than what can be held, known, or experienced in any individual life. It is larger than the known world, and it is more powerful than any force used against humanity. The kingdom is a shelter for all who come to build their nests in it. It is a place of refuge and respite. As citizens of God's kingdom, may we be safe places for others to rest.

REFLECTION

How do you see God's kingdom expanding in you? What small seeds have been placed in your heart that you have allowed to take root? How can you encourage others to grow?

My Thoughts

After reflecting on this devotion and follow-up questions, here are my thoughts.

My Response

This is how I can apply the message to my life.

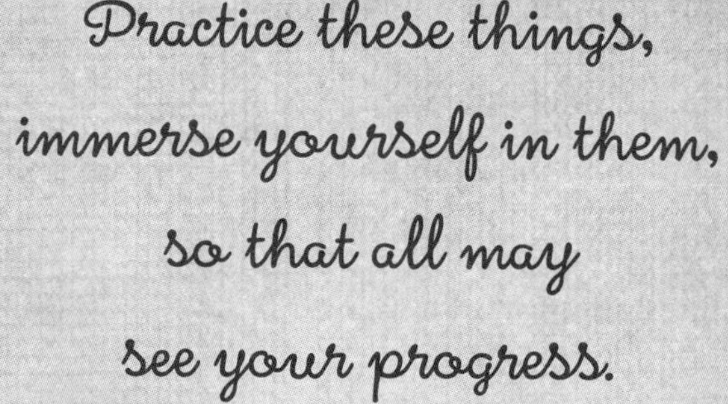

Practice these things,
immerse yourself in them,
so that all may
see your progress.

1 TIMOTHY 4:15 ESV

To me, this Scripture feels most like (check one)

☐ A PROMISE ☐ AN INSTRUCTION ☐ A TRUTH

Here's how it impacts me...

PRAYER

GRATITUDE

I have been blessed with so many good things.
Here is what I am particularly thankful for this week.

REQUESTS

After reading and reflecting, here is what I'm asking God for.

WEEK 43

LISTEN FIRST

"What are you arguing with them about?"

MARK 9:16 CSB

Instead of jumping into the middle of an argument with a lecture, Jesus asked, "What are you arguing about?" He first listened and gave them a chance to explain themselves. How often do we jump to conclusions instead of asking questions to understand before we offer perspective or advice? Jesus didn't storm in to put people in their place. Why would we?

It is worth our time, energy, and humility to carefully gauge a situation by checking in with those involved rather than making assumptions. We can follow the lead of Jesus and enter into spaces, especially ones with tensions running high, with open hearts to first listen and assess. Only then should we venture to respond.

REFLECTION

How do you respond to arguments? Can you refrain from jumping to conclusions without first listening to others? How can you become more discerning?

My Thoughts

After reflecting on this devotion and follow-up questions, here are my thoughts.

My Response

This is how I can apply the message to my life.

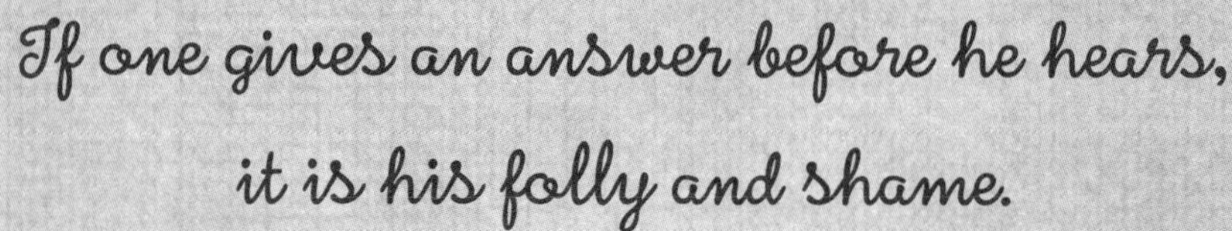

If one gives an answer before he hears,
it is his folly and shame.

PROVERBS 18:13 ESV

To me, this Scripture feels most like (check one)

☐ A PROMISE ☐ AN INSTRUCTION ☐ A TRUTH

Here's how it impacts me...

PRAYER

GRATITUDE

I have been blessed with so many good things.
Here is what I am particularly thankful for this week.

REQUESTS

After reading and reflecting, here is what I'm asking God for.

WEEK 44

IMPORTANCE OF SERVICE

"Anyone who wants to be first must be the very last, and the servant of all."

MARK 9:35 NIV

This directive was in response to the disciples arguing about which of them was the greatest. We all want favored places in the sight of others, don't we? It was no different for the disciples; they each wanted to be the best. However, Jesus said anyone who wants to be first must be willing to be the very last. He prescribed a humble, pliant attitude instead of a proud, pushy one.

How many of us take this truth to heart? If we want to be known as great, we must be willing to humble ourselves and let others go ahead of us. If we want to honor God with our lives, we must seek to serve all people. We can't pick and choose who is worthy of our generosity.

REFLECTION

The kingdom of God does not work the way the world does. How can you stop promoting yourself and spend time serving instead? What does it look like to honor God with your life?

My Thoughts

After reflecting on this devotion and follow-up questions, here are my thoughts.

My Response

This is how I can apply the message to my life.

"Everyone who exalts himself will be humbled, but the one who humbles himself will be exalted."

LUKE 18:14 NASB

To me, this Scripture feels most like (check one)

☐ A PROMISE ☐ AN INSTRUCTION ☐ A TRUTH

Here's how it impacts me…

PRAYER

GRATITUDE

I have been blessed with so many good things.
Here is what I am particularly thankful for this week.

REQUESTS

After reading and reflecting, here is what I'm asking God for.

WEEK 45

HOMECOMING

> "The son said to him, 'Father, I have sinned against heaven and before you. I am no longer worthy to be called your son.' But the father said to his servants, 'Bring quickly the best robe, and put it on him, and put a ring on his hand, and shoes on his feet.'"
>
> LUKE 15:21-22 ESV

Repentance is a beautiful act of surrender to the love of the Father. It admits we have done wrong and chooses to submit to whatever the Father has for us. We yield to his correction. We humble ourselves before him and allow him to do what he will.

Does the Father shame us when we come to our senses? Not at all. He clothes us with his own royal robes. Jesus has already offered all we need to be fully purified and made right in God's presence. We are covered in the garments of Christ, and he calls us his own. Who God says we are is more important than how we feel about ourselves, and he does not manipulate, humiliate, or destroy our hearts when we yield them to him.

REFLECTION

Where do you feel most at home? When have you felt the affection of the Father? Thank him for his kindness and compassion this week as you yield to his correction and repent.

My Thoughts

After reflecting on this devotion and follow-up questions, here are my thoughts.

My Response

This is how I can apply the message to my life.

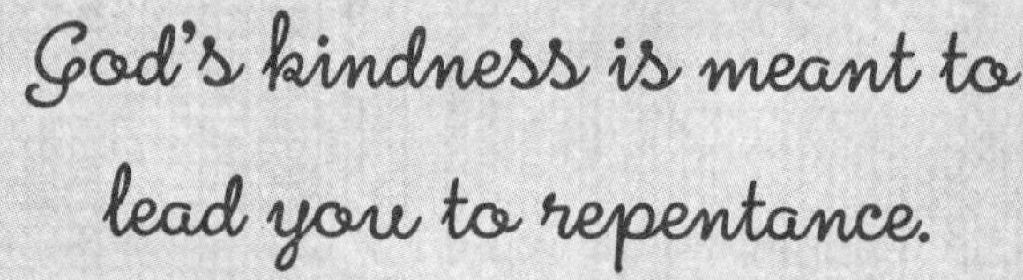

God's kindness is meant to lead you to repentance.

ROMANS 2:4 ESV

To me, this Scripture feels most like (check one)

☐ A PROMISE ☐ AN INSTRUCTION ☐ A TRUTH

Here's how it impacts me...

PRAYER

GRATITUDE

I have been blessed with so many good things.
Here is what I am particularly thankful for this week.

REQUESTS

After reading and reflecting, here is what I'm asking God for.

WEEK 46

ACTS OF COMPASSION

> "I was hungry and you gave me something to eat; I was thirsty and you gave me something to drink; I was a stranger and you took me in; I was naked and you clothed me; I was sick and you took care of me; I was in prison and you visited me."
>
> MATTHEW 25:35-36 CSB

Jesus says that when we act with practical compassion to meet others' needs, we are serving Jesus himself. Take some time to meditate on this wonderful truth. When we offer food to someone who is hungry, we can do it as if we are feeding Jesus. When we take care of the sick, welcome the stranger, and visit the lonely, each is an act of worship.

Does this change the way you look at such acts? Would it change how often you acted with practical kindness if you knew Jesus saw and received each one as if it were being done to him? Acts of compassion are not just good things to do; practices of kindness are our offering of worship to the Creator of all things.

REFLECTION

Thank God for changing you with his kindness. How can you offer your worship to him by the way you live? What does it look like to do good, act justly, and love mercy?

My Thoughts

After reflecting on this devotion and follow-up questions, here are my thoughts.

My Response

This is how I can apply the message to my life.

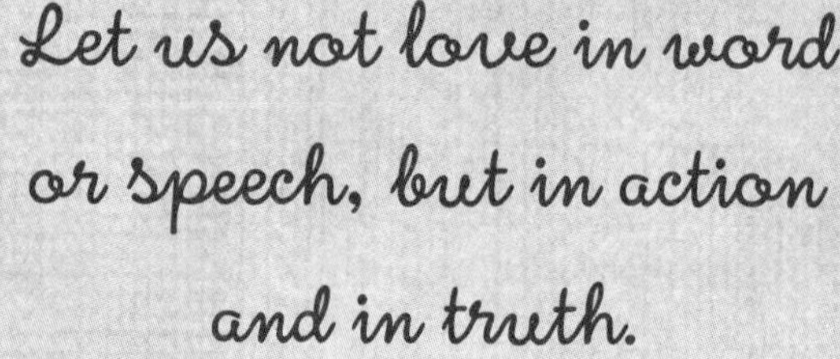

Let us not love in word or speech, but in action and in truth.

1 JOHN 3:18 CSB

To me, this Scripture feels most like (check one)

☐ A PROMISE ☐ AN INSTRUCTION ☐ A TRUTH

Here's how it impacts me...

PRAYER

GRATITUDE

I have been blessed with so many good things.
Here is what I am particularly thankful for this week.

REQUESTS

After reading and reflecting, here is what I'm asking God for.

WEEK 47

WHAT ABOUT YOU

"Who do you say that I am?"

LUKE 9:20 NASB

Regardless of who others think Jesus is, who do you say he is? It's a question each of us must answer. Our parents can't do it for us; neither can our partners. Our friends can't carry our faith. We are seen and known for who we are and what we believe. Jesus will not overlook even one of us.

What you believe matters. It affects every area of your life. Your thoughts, actions, and intentions work together to produce a life built on your values. Take this opportunity to evaluate and choose how you want to live. The present moment is when the power of your choices matters. Don't put off for tomorrow what can be done today.

REFLECTION

Who is Jesus to you? How can you know him more? How is his life reflected in yours? What can you do to honor his name this week?

My Thoughts

After reflecting on this devotion and follow-up questions, here are my thoughts.

My Response

This is how I can apply the message to my life.

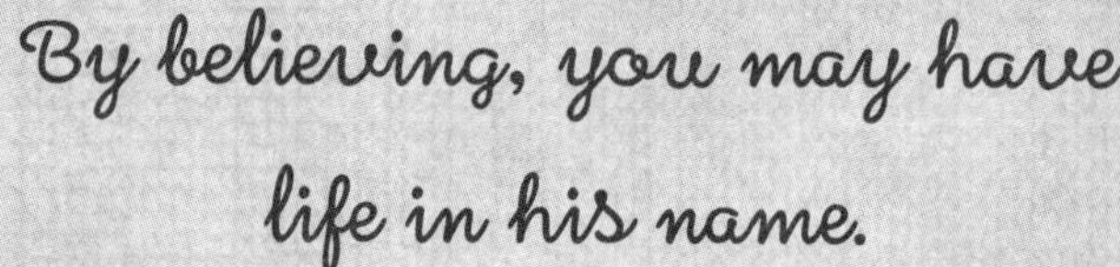

By believing, you may have life in his name.

JOHN 20:31 NCV

To me, this Scripture feels most like (check one)

☐ A PROMISE ☐ AN INSTRUCTION ☐ A TRUTH

Here's how it impacts me...

PRAYER

GRATITUDE

I have been blessed with so many good things.
Here is what I am particularly thankful for this week.

REQUESTS

After reading and reflecting, here is what I'm asking God for.

WEEK 48

OASIS OF PEACE

"Come to me, all of you who are weary and carry heavy burdens, and I will give you rest."

MATTHEW 11:28 NLT

Every day has the possibility of taking on new, heavy burdens. There are diseases spreading, mental health crises happening, wars, rumors of wars, and the struggle to live in a world where prices and economic strain make it harder to get by. There are so many reasons to worry! And yet, Jesus says we can take our burdens to him. He promises to refresh us in the living waters of his presence.

Every time a burden weighs you down, come to Jesus. Give him the heavy load no matter how little or how long you have been carrying it. He will do the heavy lifting for you. He is a good God, a gracious friend, and a faithful help. Rest in his presence and come alive in his love today.

REFLECTION

Thank Jesus for being your oasis of peace. What burdens do you need to bring to him right now? Ask him to fill you with the comfort of his presence and revive your weary heart.

My Thoughts

After reflecting on this devotion and follow-up questions, here are my thoughts.

My Response

This is how I can apply the message to my life.

It is for freedom that Christ has set us free. Do not let yourselves be burdened again by a yoke of slavery.

GALATIANS 5:1 NIV

To me, this Scripture feels most like (check one)

☐ A PROMISE ☐ AN INSTRUCTION ☐ A TRUTH

Here's how it impacts me…

PRAYER

GRATITUDE

I have been blessed with so many good things.
Here is what I am particularly thankful for this week.

REQUESTS

After reading and reflecting, here is what I'm asking God for.

WEEK 49

A LIGHTER LOAD

"The burden that I ask you to accept is easy; the load I give you to carry is light."

MATTHEW 11:30 NCV

When Jesus asks us to partner with him, it doesn't mean we get to opt out of our responsibilities or choices. The load he asks us to carry, however, is light. It is not too much. When we offer our heavy burdens to Jesus, he willingly takes them. What he offers in return is easy for us to bear.

After you lay down your burdens at Jesus' feet and receive the rest and refreshment of his Spirit, he offers you something to carry. What is the light load he offers you? Is it to be kind to those who challenge you today? Is it to refuse to fight with someone unwilling to listen to you? Whatever it is, accept it with gratitude and joy today, for it is much better than what you traded in.

REFLECTION

Accept what Jesus is offering today! Thank him for the rest and refreshing peace of his tender care. What load has he asked you to hand over to him? What are your responsibilities?

My Thoughts

After reflecting on this devotion and follow-up questions, here are my thoughts.

My Response

This is how I can apply the message to my life.

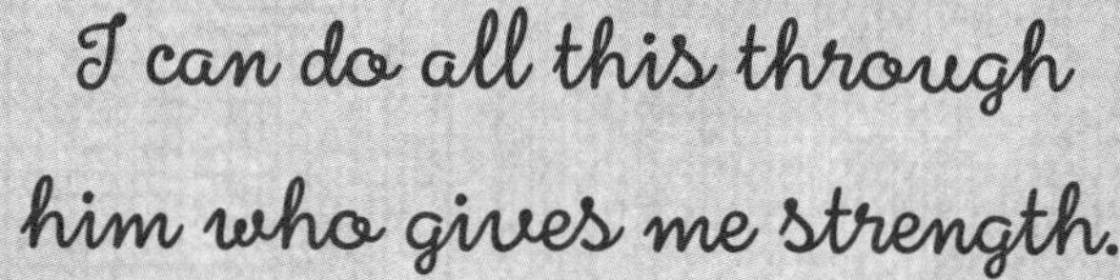

I can do all this through
him who gives me strength.

PHILIPPIANS 4:13 NIV

To me, this Scripture feels most like (check one)

☐ A PROMISE ☐ AN INSTRUCTION ☐ A TRUTH

Here's how it impacts me...

PRAYER

GRATITUDE

I have been blessed with so many good things.
Here is what I am particularly thankful for this week.

REQUESTS

After reading and reflecting, here is what I'm asking God for.

WEEK 50

A NARROW PATH

"Make every effort to enter through the narrow door, because I tell you, many will try to enter and won't be able."

LUKE 13:24 CSB

There is a cost to enter the narrow door of God's kingdom. It is not easy to choose the pathway of God's love, for it requires dying to self. It requires continued humility. If we want to feast in the kingdom of heaven, we need to become like children, learning from Christ and putting aside what we thought we already knew from tradition.

If you humble yourself before God, let his guidance direct you, and stay softhearted in his love, he will lead you in the way of his everlasting life. Don't let swelling pride keep you from being small enough to enter. Lay down the things that keep you stuck and yield to Jesus' gentle leadership.

REFLECTION

Don't waste your life on your own agenda. How can you live with God's love as the primary banner over your life? What does choosing the narrow way look like for you?

My Thoughts

After reflecting on this devotion and follow-up questions, here are my thoughts.

My Response

This is how I can apply the message to my life.

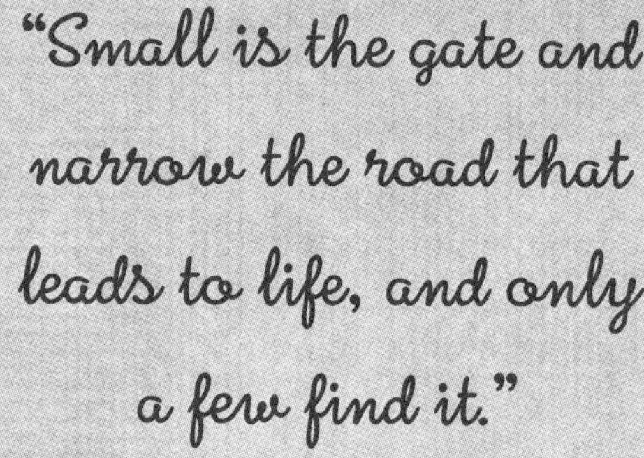

"Small is the gate and narrow the road that leads to life, and only a few find it."

MATTHEW 7:14 NIV

To me, this Scripture feels most like (check one)

☐ A PROMISE ☐ AN INSTRUCTION ☐ A TRUTH

Here's how it impacts me...

PRAYER

GRATITUDE

I have been blessed with so many good things.
Here is what I am particularly thankful for this week.

REQUESTS

After reading and reflecting, here is what I'm asking God for.

WEEK 51

MORE IMPORTANT THINGS

"My food is to do the will of Him who sent Me, and to finish His work."

JOHN 4:34 NKJV

The disciples were concerned that Jesus hadn't eaten anything. Jesus was focused, not on filling his belly, but on doing what God had sent him to do. Though the disciples meant well, Jesus was preoccupied with ministering to the people flocking to hear him speak.

Jesus could sense his time was limited. Don't we feel that when we're on a deadline? As Ecclesiastes says, there is a time to work and a time to rest. A time to sow and a time to reap. Jesus saw the harvest of people coming to him, and he knew it was time to work. May we also sense the spiritual seasons and give energy to what needs it in the moment. Sometimes, the most important thing to do is feed ourselves and rest; other times, it's serving those who come to us.

REFLECTION

Are you willing to do the will of the Father over other desires? What are you called to give energy to in this season? What is most important right now?

My Thoughts

After reflecting on this devotion and follow-up questions, here are my thoughts.

My Response

This is how I can apply the message to my life.

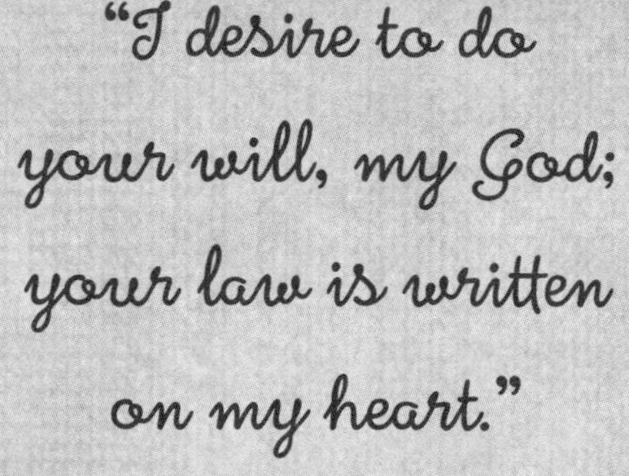

"I desire to do
your will, my God;
your law is written
on my heart."

PSALM 40:8 NIV

To me, this Scripture feels most like (check one)

☐ A PROMISE ☐ AN INSTRUCTION ☐ A TRUTH

Here's how it impacts me...

PRAYER

GRATITUDE

I have been blessed with so many good things.
Here is what I am particularly thankful for this week.

REQUESTS

After reading and reflecting, here is what I'm asking God for.

WEEK 52

GREATEST COMMANDMENT

> "Love the Lord your God with all your heart and with all your soul and with all your mind and with all your strength."
>
> MARK 12:30 NIV

The greatest commandment is not an invitation to rigidity but to devotion. As we love the Lord with the passion of our hearts, the energy of our being, the thoughts within us, and every bit of strength, it becomes the core of our why. Why are we kind to others? Because we love the Lord. Why extend grace when others would ridicule or dismiss? Because of our love for God.

Is love the driving force of your faith? If not, take some time to connect to God through his Spirit. We love because God first loved us. No matter how lacking we are in any moment, we need only receive the abundant love that Christ offers us first. When we are filled with his love, it will overflow from us.

REFLECTION

Thank God for his perfect love. How do your heart, thoughts, and actions reflect the passion of God's love in your life? Is the greatest commandment your driving force? How does devotion differ from perfection?

My Thoughts

After reflecting on this devotion and follow-up questions, here are my thoughts.

My Response

This is how I can apply the message to my life.

"You shall love the Lord your God with all your heart and with all your soul and with all your might."

DEUTERONOMY 6:5 ESV

To me, this Scripture feels most like (check one)

☐ A PROMISE ☐ AN INSTRUCTION ☐ A TRUTH

Here's how it impacts me...

PRAYER

GRATITUDE

I have been blessed with so many good things.
Here is what I am particularly thankful for this week.

REQUESTS

After reading and reflecting, here is what I'm asking God for.

Prayer Requests

	DATE	WHAT I AM BELIEVING FOR	HOW AND WHEN GOD ANSWERED

Prayer Requests

	DATE	WHAT I AM BELIEVING FOR	HOW AND WHEN GOD ANSWERED

Prayer Requests

	DATE	WHAT I AM BELIEVING FOR	HOW AND WHEN GOD ANSWERED

Prayer Requests

	DATE	WHAT I AM BELIEVING FOR	HOW AND WHEN GOD ANSWERED

Prayer Requests

	DATE	WHAT I AM BELIEVING FOR	HOW AND WHEN GOD ANSWERED

Prayer Requests

	DATE	WHAT I AM BELIEVING FOR	HOW AND WHEN GOD ANSWERED

Prayer Requests

	DATE	WHAT I AM BELIEVING FOR	HOW AND WHEN GOD ANSWERED

Prayer Requests

	DATE	WHAT I AM BELIEVING FOR	HOW AND WHEN GOD ANSWERED

Prayer Requests

	DATE	WHAT I AM BELIEVING FOR	HOW AND WHEN GOD ANSWERED

Prayer Requests

	DATE	WHAT I AM BELIEVING FOR	HOW AND WHEN GOD ANSWERED

Prayer Requests

	DATE	WHAT I AM BELIEVING FOR	HOW AND WHEN GOD ANSWERED